REAL LIFE

Endorsements for *Real Life*

"*Real Life* is for all who seek a successful, fulfilling, meaningful career. The individual stories are so inspiring. The book should become a university text book … an important 'self help' publication. My speeches on leadership include quotes from these individuals, and Tom's assessment of how they achieved success."

— Dr. Jimmy Simmons, President Emeritus
Lamar University, Beaumont, Texas

"This book is filled with proven principles and practices that lead towards a path of success in business, and success in LIFE, period. The inspiring accounts from individuals of many different backgrounds—educationally, financially, culturally, and personally—inspire and enhance everyday wisdom that is translatable to our own lives. The core principle is to show up and never give up!"

— Suzanne Frazier, retired social worker, family therapist

"There are many books on finding a career path, how to succeed, leadership et al, but *Real Life* takes a unique approach with the personal stories of individuals, and their advice. I like their emphasis on "find another path" when one path isn't working. It helps people remember there are many paths to a goal. The book has many solid principles as take-aways."

—Dory Beatrice & Associates, Clinical Social Work

REAL LIFE

Real life career success stories
and advice to help you chart
your own course

THOMAS V. BROWN

Sunset Cove Press
Gig Harbor, Washington

Printed in the United States of America.

Library of Congress Control Number: 2016907605

Sunset Cove Press, Gig Harbor, WA

ISBN 978-0-9973860-0-4

Acknowledgements

First, many thanks to the 17 successful contributors who made this book possible by sharing their career stories, advice, and observations. Their candor, insight, and help was invaluable. Thanks to my granddaughter, Ingrid Brown, for encouraging me by being a gifted author, artist and storyteller while still in grade school. Sarah, my wife and partner for more than 50 years, proofed every word and provided advice, support and suggestions and helped me through the rough spots. I was lucky to find Cheryl Feeney, my editor and publishing coach, who transformed my writing into something resembling a book, and did a great job of dealing with all the tedious but necessary steps in the publishing process.

Contents

Introduction

The purpose of this book is to show how you can succeed in your chosen career. To write it, I collected the stories of dozens of contributors, friends, and colleagues who achieved success, and included comments from my own life experiences. Through analysis, observations and comparisons, the advice given allows readers to evaluate their own career paths and identify and develop skills and experience to achieve success.

To begin, we must define career success. Most of us will spend 30 to 40 years in a series of jobs, and with all of that time invested we should have some pretty clear goals for what we expect to achieve. As a practical matter, enough money should be accumulated to finance the last 30 or 40 years of our lives—after retirement. This won't be easy. Healthier lifestyles and modern medicine have given us longer lifespans; however, as we age, we are at increased risk of a host of ailments that can require very expensive care.

This book does not address the challenges of aging, but it does describe how 17 people achieved success in their careers through solid preparation, desperate need, determination, persistence, and, in almost every case, hard work. Their stories offer a glimpse into various careers in business, education, the Armed Services, professions in corporations, and public service. There are successful people who start with, and stick with, a prestigious company, like in Aryna Swope's story in Chapter 9. There are successful people, like

Kent Weymouth in Chapter 19, who were never employed by a leading company. There are also successful people who never sought a job with companies like GE or Microsoft, like my friend Bill Brown, who knew what he wanted—a job as head football coach at a California high school.

My hope is that this compilation of real life experiences will assist in exploring different careers, choosing one you will really enjoy, and also show how to prepare effectively and become motivated to perform—every day—an outstanding job. Learn from their experiences how to maximize the payoff in executing an effective plan so you can enjoy a comfortable and secure retirement, and feel proud of what you accomplished during all those years in the working world.

1

What is Success?

After years of hard work, you've earned a bachelor's degree, perhaps completed a master's program, or received certification in a technical field. Now what? How do you move into your chosen career and onto the road to success?

This book is a compilation of the knowledge shared by people with proven success stories. How they did it. Real people with real professions who were willing to share with me the pitfalls and victories they experienced throughout their chosen careers. The one thing they have in common: they achieved success and now enjoy the life they imagined. After you read their stories, you will see many different paths to success, and many different kinds of people who have become successful.

The book does not deal with the meaning of life or how

to choose the best career for your particular skills and interests, or how to find the perfect job. It does propose different strategies and tactics that can be applied to achieve goals in the career of your choice. The road to success is not always smooth. The contributors talked about the obstacles, failures, disappointments, bad luck, and scholastic difficulties they experienced, all of which they found ways to overcome. But before we discuss the failures and successes of my outstanding contributors, let's spend some time discussing what success is, and what it isn't.

My professional career lasted almost 50 years. Now that I am retired, my wife and I pay for expenses using the investments and savings we accumulated during our working careers. It is easy for me to take a long view of career success now, but when I was starting out, career success was harder to define. One lesson I learned—a lesson I emphasize to people beginning a career—is this: much of what you hear about career success is baloney.

Here are some of the misleading or false definitions of success you may run into—what career success is not.

Career success is not landing a job with a prestigious employer. Hired by GE or Proctor & Gamble or Google or Microsoft does not guarantee career success. Early in your career, develop confidence by learning the ropes, working hard, and figuring out how to accomplish things of value to your employer. Big companies offer excellent training, advancement opportunities, and well-defined career paths, but they can also have complicated political environments, boring work assigned to junior employees, and a talent surplus, which means many talented, qualified employees compete for every promotion. So if for some reason you find yourself being turned down by a prestigious employer, or the big corporate environment doesn't appeal to you, don't become discouraged. Just find another path to your career success.

Career success is not defined by an impressive job title. Not all management trainees go on to become members of a management team. Some organizations have legions of assistant vice presidents, deputy directors and senior administrators. No job title is nearly as important as the contribution an individual makes to the success of an organization. Your boss, or the leader of your team or work unit—the person you report to—is not measured by how many senior administrators he or she has on her team. She is measured on how much wood her woodchucks chuck. And she evaluates her employees the same way.

Don't be faked out by job titles. Learn the hierarchy of the company. Know your boss, his or her boss, and who runs the organization. You need to know who will evaluate your performance, and how that will be done. Have a clear understanding of how you can contribute towards your organization's success, and then get to work and show management how much wood the woodchuck can chuck.

Career success is not the same as achieving a target salary. When I graduated from college and started my career, I earned slightly less than $6,000 that first year—roughly the equivalent of $46,000 in today's market. The conventional wisdom at the time was that achieving an income of

$10,000 per year, which I hoped to reach within a few years, would mark me as a success and guarantee a prosperous life. Five years later I was working at IBM, making considerably more than $10,000, but the game had changed. The goal for the really fast-trackers was to make your age: reach a wage of $30,000 by your 30th birthday. I didn't make it, although I was close.

Many career employees today earn enough to cover the rent or mortgage, buy food and make car payments, and perhaps splurge too much on sporting gear, eating out, vacations, and clothes. What's missing is long-range financial planning—savings accounts, investments, home equity—whatever it takes to accumulate enough wealth to pay for comfort, security and to live a good life once we decide to stop earning a paycheck.

Don't be faked out by a high starting salary or by a job that promises high potential earnings. Make career choices based on the best fit for your interests, talents, and abilities, then develop a plan to achieve success and earn the payoff you will need to live well in retirement.

So, what *is* career success? The conclusion I reached after interviewing people for this book is this: measuring it has a lot to do with how well they developed and executed plans that allow them to fully enjoy life by their 70th birthday.

They experienced failures and inevitable setbacks, and recovered to enjoy a chosen career. They are able to look back with gratitude for the opportunities they had to learn and to grow, professionally and as a person. They are satisfied that they earned the right to play on some very successful teams. Many took the opportunity to mentor, train, lead, manage or build a team, organization, company or legacy.

The path to success varies. Some of the people interviewed had enormous investments in education and preparation; others had very little preparation but a great deal of determination, or even desperation. All succeeded. Their hope in sharing their experiences is to inspire each of you to choose the right career and work hard to achieve success.

Three basic key elements came to the forefront while interviewing the contributors:

1. Understand an organization's goals.
2. Learn when to raise your hand.
3. Be smart about money.

In most organizations, leadership does a pretty good job of articulating top-level goals. In the 1970s, IBM's goal was to grow the business to $100 billion in annual revenues. When we created strategic goals at Xircom in the early 1990s, the first was to become the leading provider of network adapters for portable computers. For many employees, hearing goals like these seemed far removed from what they were doing every day—a long way from the wood the woodchuck was chucking every day.

While strategic planning and goals are an important function of leadership, for an individual employee it may be more important to have a very clear picture of what goals and challenges his boss has signed up for. If you know that your boss needs to recruit, hire, and train ten workers to support a new product launch scheduled for the following year, find ways to help achieve the goal. If you don't know what the goals are in your department, find out and develop a plan to help accomplish them. Do this successfully once, and you will establish confidence that your participation can make a difference—solid contributions towards achieving important business goals. Team players reap rewards.

You have personal goals and career goals. Learn how and when to express them. Many organizations expect management to assist employees in creating professional development plans. Some managers don't enjoy this requirement of their position, and not all excel in mentoring employees. Failure to craft a suitable career plan isn't entirely management's fault. Many employees think in terms of how long before the next raise or promotion to the next rung on the ladder, instead of in terms of a career.

Are you carrying your share of the load? Are you making a positive contribution to the success of the organization? And are you spending time and energy each day trying to help your boss solve the toughest problems?

Let's say you have been in your job for nine months or so. Your manager is required to give you a formal, written performance appraisal after your first 12 months, also the time when career planning and employee development are discussed. This creates an opportunity for the exceptional employee to present well-thought out plans to management. Prepare for the performance review, and at the same time help your manager with the process. List your accomplishments, the skills developed, lessons learned, and training that you have experienced in your first 12 months. Prior to your review, present the document to your manager, let him know how much you appreciate being part of his team, and that you look forward to discussing your self-evaluation during your performance review.

When the time comes for the review, be pro-active and prepared. Identify opportunities for professional growth in the organization and ask for advice in how to prepare for your future with the company. Be specific when stating your goals, and discuss with your manager how to achieve them. If you want to lead a team on a significant project or to become a regional sales representative, ask what specific steps to take to meet the requirements.

Setting career goals is your job; advising on how to prepare and what assignments to complete to reach your goals is your manager's job. Be prepared to raise your hand, state your goals, and follow the development plan, and you will be far ahead of most of your peers. And the most likely to advance in the department.

Finally, it is never too early to establish a financial plan that will allow you to live comfortably once the paychecks end. Set goals that will pay off a mortgage during working years. Start saving early, be smart about money, and continue to enjoy life after your career.

Now let's learn how seventeen people made plans, adjusted their plans, or, in some cases changed to a completely different path, and are enjoying the payoff.

2

C. J. Berwick

World's happiest seafood tycoon

By her early 70s, C.J. Berwick cut back her work week to around 20 to 30 hours spent between her two restaurants, The Fish House and Encore, in Key Largo, Florida. C.J. has a smile in her voice as she talks about her business: the 50 plus employees, some of whom go back to the start of her business in 1987; her lovely cookbooks; celebrity customers, a long list which includes Jimmy Buffet and Paul Newman; and the many friends she has made among customers, vendors, fishermen and staff. Both restaurants are successful, and the cookbook, *Exceptional Florida Keys Cuisine*, dedicated to the Wyland Foundation and bearing a spectacular Wyland painting of undersea life on its cover, is in its second edition.

In 2014, C.J. and her partner restructured the corporate

organization so the restaurants can continue after she fully retires; the employees and management can earn stock in the business and become owners. When I interviewed C.J., she was excited about handing out year-end employee bonuses—serious money in the thousands—for many staff members. She is also proud that she can pay a good wage, a living wage for a family.

C.J. is one of the happiest, most contented entrepreneurs I have ever met. It is remarkable, perhaps even close to a miracle, that she found career success in the restaurant business in Key Largo—neither she nor her partner had restaurant experience. She didn't start on The Fish House until she was in her mid-40s, and although she held responsible positions in a variety of businesses, she discovered running a successful restaurant was a lot of work.

She described getting to know the business:

> I was familiar with human resources, insurance, and accounting. We jumped in and quickly realized that the business required long hours—9:00 a.m. until midnight, including every holiday and weekend—creativity, patience, attention to detail, people skills, personnel skills, community involvement and more.

Asked why she chose the restaurant business, which has a terrifying failure rate for start-ups, she answered that she wanted a people business, something in the hospitality field. She and her family had moved to Key Largo from elsewhere in Florida and found it to be a relaxed, very pleasant and laid back place. She envisioned a restaurant serving high-quality local seafood in an attractive resort environment, away from the fast pace of Miami and environs. She studied nutrition in college and was interested in food. This all sounds logical: she was living in a place that seemed like a good location for a new restaurant, she was attracted to the hospitality industry, liked working with people, and had acquired valuable general business experience from her previous jobs.

Now let's take a look at C.J.'s life story to learn how she acquired the determination, work ethic, confidence, and people skills to create a successful career in such a difficult field.

C.J.'s dad was a career Navy officer who was at sea serving on an aircraft carrier the day she was born. Navy life took the family from the east coast to California and back. She credits her parents for her strong work ethic. C.J. says they were "supportive but strict" and taught her basic lessons about what it takes to succeed: "Get to work on time. Study hard. And work hard." She credits her early work experience as a valuable foundation for her entrepreneurial career.

From the time she was a teenager until she moved to Key Largo, C.J. worked and gained life skills that led to her ultimate career as a restaurant owner. She worked in retail in high school, and learned she didn't like it. She spent three months touring Europe with a couple of girlfriends. She attended Montgomery College in Maryland and Murray State University in Kentucky, where she majored in biology and business while working three part-time jobs. She married and raised two children (one now works at The Fish House).

Early in their marriage, she and her husband relocated to Long Island where she worked for five years as a medical secretary—a job she landed because of her college science classes. They returned to Kentucky and she worked at Murray State while taking college classes and being a wife and mother. C.J. learned a great deal from several professors at Murray State who mentored and helped her to expand her knowledge of business.

In the early 1970s, she moved with her family to Florida, first to Clearwater, where C.J. was employed as an office manager, and later to Stuart, where she was benefits manager in a 350-bed hospital. She developed a deep appreciation for the importance of positive human resources policies and practices in the very competitive hospital sector. She believes employee benefits are a powerful motivator—all employees at her restaurants receive three-weeks paid vacation every year, which is considered very generous in this industry.

After nine years in Stuart, she and her family moved to Key Largo and entered the restaurant business. In addition to the experience acquired during the 23 years she worked prior to opening The Fish House, and the mentoring at Murray State, C.J. found the Business and Professional Women's Association was a valuable source of support and help. She was also active in the local Chamber of Commerce, and believes that community involvement was a key ingredient in her business success.

When I asked what advice she would give people just starting out, her list was short:

- Work hard at developing people skills.

- Get all the education you can, especially in economics and accounting, if you plan for a career in business.

- Volunteer in a potential career field while still in school so you can try it out.

- Find the work you have a passion for, then enjoy it!

C.J.'s restaurants have powerful appeal. To see what I mean, go to www.fishhouse.com and browse around. Even from 3,000 miles away, I can almost feel myself relaxing in a comfortable chair at the Fish House and ordering a drink to enjoy as I study the menu, and can almost smell the pan-fried fresh fish, and taste the Key Lime pie.

The restaurant's website states: "All of our dishes are served in a fun, friendly, and casual 'Keys-style' atmosphere." That "Keys-style" atmosphere is important, and not just for the customers. C.J. tells a delightful story about the laid back life at The Fish House in Key Largo.

> Years ago we recruited a woman from an executive position in Philadelphia to come to Key Largo to become general manager of The Fish House. She arrived in Key Largo driving her black BMW, the car filled with career clothes, high heels, and cosmetics.

> Now she drives a white Honda with a fishing pole in the back, and when she arrives at work, the first thing she does is kick off her shoes and slip on her flip-flops!

C.J. obviously enjoys telling this story, and by the time she is at the end she is chuckling in her own warm, friendly way. Listening to her describe the last 25 years in the restaurant business gives a very clear image of a person who worked hard, loves her work, and found great success in her chosen career.

3

Coach Bill Brown

Life is an Interview

His first name is Coach, as many of his friends still call him, even though he retired nearly fifteen years ago after 38 years of teaching and coaching in high schools and community colleges in Southern California. Today Coach Bill lives in a beautiful home in a well-tended community in Washington State, organizes weekly golf games with his pals, plans frequent trips in the United States and overseas, and enjoys cooking gourmet meals and discovering new restaurants. In his mid-70s and enjoying good health, he is the very picture of a successful coach and teacher.

But when Bill was a junior at Indiana State, his career goal was much different. He was holding what he thought was a winning hand, planning to graduate the following year and enroll in medical school to become a doctor. He was counting on the family business—an Indiana packaging company—for the funding necessary to support him in medical school and during residencies and internships. When the packaging business went bust during his third year in college, Bill knew that was a game-changer. He folded the hand he thought was a winner and turned his focus on becoming a teacher and coach. On becoming head coach of a high school football team. On becoming "Coach Brown".

It wasn't a hard decision to make. Bill had always enjoyed sports and he excelled at basketball and football. The idea of earning a living doing something he loved was appealing. At age 21, he graduated from Indiana State and within days he was pounding the pavements of Orange County in Southern California, looking for a teaching job. There were only two problems: first, with the exception of some valuable mentoring during his student teaching semester at Indiana State, he really didn't know much about teaching; second, with no coaching experience, he knew no one would hire him as a high school coach. So he made the best of a weak hand and took a job teaching physical education in a junior high school, where he stayed for six years, learning and organizing his career plan.

During Bill's first semester in college, he had the good fortune of taking an economics class from a professor who really impressed him. Bill described him as being extremely organized. Each day, the teacher outlined his lesson on the blackboard, and students who had a goal of earning an A in the class, like Bill, would copy the outline into their notes.

You could probably describe this professor using many different, but accurate terms: he probably excelled at preparation; he seemed to have mastered his subject in detail; and he most likely had a philosophy of teaching that included everything he could to help his students succeed.

In his early years as a teacher, Bill also learned a lot from a basketball coach who developed detailed plans and processes for coaching. Bill also described the coach as being organized.

During his early years teaching junior high physical education, Bill kept his goal in focus. He wanted to move up to a coaching position in a high school, and the position he wanted was head football coach. That meant he needed another 30 hours of graduate level classes to meet California requirements for teaching high school. He applied for, and received, a graduate assistantship at Indiana State. This financial aid package, plus what he had on hand from cashing in his retirement accounts, financed another year of school. He earned a master's degree in education and returned to Southern California.

It sounds hard, doesn't it, to leave California, go back to school in Indiana, sacrifice your retirement savings, live like a student once again with tests, term papers, grades, and the grind of successfully completing 30 hours of graduate level classes in one academic year. I'm sure it was difficult, but a goal-oriented person who wants to change his first name to Coach doesn't see another year of graduate school as an impossible challenge, if that is what is needed to get to the goal. Bill needed to do that, and so he did. He was ready to start moving towards becoming a head football coach and build a successful high school football program.

Bill was back in California and one step closer to his goal, landing a teaching job at Orange High School where he signed up to coach the freshman football team. He also began working on skills needed as a head coach:

» Organization

» Planning

» Develop a coaching philosophy

» Motivate students and coaching staff

» Be prepared

» Hard work

At this point I want to describe in some detail Bill's views on motivation, how it relates to achieving goals and personal responsibility. Bill believes there are three sources of motivation:

Rewards. Fear. Self-motivation.

Of these three, he identifies self-motivation as clearly the most valuable and powerful. Random House Dictionary defines self-motivation as "initiative to undertake or continue a task or activity without another's prodding or supervision." This certainly fits all the hard work and effort Bill put in to achieve his goal of a head coach position, but self-motivation was also an important element of his coaching philosophy, closely related to the core concept of personal responsibility.

Each year, Bill stated the rules to his coaching staff and his players. "These are the only rules that apply to my team members: Do right. Do wrong, and you get punished. The nature of the punishment depends on the circumstances."

He would go on to explain that each individual knows the difference between right and wrong, and each person is responsible for making their own choices in life. If you want to succeed, then choose to succeed. Set appropriate goals and work hard to attain those goals. Bill followed the philosophy that a coach's job is to help each team member develop the skills needed to succeed. To achieve significant goals, to exceed what you thought were your limits, to reach elite levels, you must be self-motivated and focused on your goals.

After a year of volunteer duty coaching the freshman football team, Bill was rewarded with an appointment to defensive coordinator for the varsity. This gave him solid credentials and the experience needed to compete for the job he wanted as head football coach. But in addition to coaching experience, he also had to understand and master the recruiting and selection process.

At that time in Orange County, California, the selection process for a high school head coach revolved around an Interview committee composed of five or six faculty members appointed by the school principal. Bill decided to become the best interviewee that any search committee had ever met. He developed a plan.

Before each interview, Bill researched the teachers on the committee to learn their names, tenure at the school, subject focus, and anything else he could turn up. He conducted practice interviews with other teachers to get experience and feedback. He anticipated the topics and questions an interview committee might cover, and created a list of topics he prepared to discuss. He handed out copies of this list at the beginning of an interview and invited the search team to question him on any of them. He also prepared position papers, write-ups on topics like team discipline, rules, or fund raising, and offered these as handouts as well. His plan included interviewing for every available high school coaching job in Southern California.

It took Bill eight years of coaching and teaching at Orange High before he reached his goal of being picked as head football coach. He accepted the position at John Glenn High School in Norwalk, California. I asked him how many interviews he participated in before he reached his goal. He replied, "Seventy-one."

Now that he had earned the job he wanted, Coach Brown had to get organized and build a successful record. He attended coaching seminars and coaches' association meetings for years, and discussed what he learned with other coaches and mentors. At one meeting, he met a colleague for breakfast and his friend showed up with another friend, the legendary Ohio State coach, Woody Hayes. For Bill, listening to Woody Hayes expound for an hour, sitting right across from him at the breakfast table, was an experience he will never forget. Bill remembers, in particular, that Woody talked mainly about history, not football; he was a great student of history.

Bill was developing a philosophy of coaching, of building a program, and because he was a thoughtful, detail-oriented person, he needed a well-thought out, detailed and documented plan. His goal was to define the system, teach the system to the dozen or so coaches on his staff, and also to the 120 boys who turned out each year, willing to work, sweat, strain, and push themselves past their limits. They trusted him as their coach to teach the skills they needed to succeed. He planned each practice with a specific agenda, and taught his coaches how to follow the plan. He also learned that plans have to be adjusted continually.

Planning was clearly a large part of being organized for Coach Brown. It became one of Bill's signature skills. One technique he developed could be used by anyone:

- Make a list of things you want to accomplish for the week, and break it down by day.

- Take a few minutes each Sunday to make a list of projects you expect to work on or complete, in the coming week.

- On a daily basis, make another list of what you commit to accomplish the following day.

- Each night, review your list for that day, and make a new list for the following day.

- Update your weekly list by crossing off the tasks you completed, and add new tasks.

When my granddaughter, Ingrid, started her 5th grade school year, she decided her elementary school needed a school newspaper, and asked for her teacher's help. The teacher became the editor and Ingrid became one of four or five reporters and cartoonists. Each reporter was given an assigned story to write for the paper. I asked Ingrid who decided what story each reporter would write. She answered, "I did. The newspaper was my idea, so I got to make the decisions."

Coach Brown had similar ideas about leadership. "I like to do what I like to do. To do this I need to be in charge."

His strategy for being in charge included, of course, reaching his goal of being head football coach, but he was also committed to setting an example of hard work. He made it a point to be first in the office every day and the last one to leave, even as an assistant coach. Bill's objective was to show his staff, and his players, that he believed that to be good at what you do, you have to be thorough and work hard at it. Bill found it gratifying when his assistants began competing with him to be the first at work in the mornings.

An element of his philosophy which explains the importance of hard work can be found in this quote: "To me, life is a race. If you stop, you lose. You have to keep working hard at getting better."

To sum up Coach Brown's approach to his career: he made choices easily, and once he made a career choice (teaching), he began setting goals (such as, becoming the best prepared candidate any search committee had ever seen) to reach his ultimate goal—head coach. Bill is the kind of person who set a goal of earning an A in every class; the kind of person who wants to enjoy his work, not just endure it for the money or perks. His approach to life clearly shows how goal-setting, self-motivation, planning, preparation, and hard work are connected to success.

The Measurement of Coach Brown's Success

The first week of June 2015, Coach Bill Brown and his wife, Suzanne, traveled from Washington to Southern California to attend a memorial service for Ted, an old friend of Bill's, a fellow coach. The service was held in the gym of Century High School, where Bill and Ted had both been head football coaches.

Bill and Suzanne had been married just a few years by June 2015. Bill was a widower, and retired, when he met Suzanne. She had never known him during his coaching career, when he earned his title, "Coach."

When Ted and Bill first met, Ted was a troubled young man with health problems, which developed into diabetes with serious complications. Ted had no plans, no career, no prospects. Bill mentored him, took him on as an assistant coach, taught him the coaching business, and when Bill went to Century High School as head football coach, he brought Ted along as an assistant. Bill then retired and Ted became head football coach, even though he was confined to a wheelchair due to his medical problems. Ted was a stand-out coach, but his health deteriorated and he passed away at age 57.

That day in June the gym was packed, primarily with students, and also men in their 30s and early 40s. Bill was scheduled to speak and he had written a speech, but his turn on the stage was late in the program and by the time he rose to walk to the microphone he had decided to ad-lib his remarks and speak from his heart.

As he was announced and began walking to the stage the crowd broke out in shouts which became a chant: "Coach! Coach! Coach!..." He delivered his piece about his friend, which was well received. His remarks included a tribute to Ted along with a lot of humor.

After the service was over, Bill and Suzanne were mobbed by a crowd of 20- to 40- year-old men, some hugging him, some lining up to have a picture taken with The Coach. One man said that Bill had saved his life by diverting him from Barrio gang life to a place on the football team—where you followed the rules, supported your team, or you didn't get to play. Suzanne learned from these men that Bill had become the father figure in the lives of these Barrio kids, many of whom grew up without fathers.

"He loved us," they told her, "but he made the rules and he enforced them. He showed us what it was to be a man."

Bill retired from coaching 15 years earlier, when he was 61 years old. Coaching high school football did not make him rich financially, but for Coach Brown, he had achieved success.

To explore a career in teaching, most school districts offer opportunities that are valuable in determining whether teaching is a good fit. Communities in Schools is a national organization that encourages adults and teens to volunteer to tutor and mentor elementary school students in math and reading. Having done this for several years for the chapter serving my local school district, I can tell you that minimum qualifications are required to deliver much needed help to these students.

Another possibility is the after-school tutoring programs offered at Boys & Girls Clubs across the country. In our community, high school seniors and college students often volunteer at the local Boys & Girls Club to help younger students with homework assignments and recreational activities after school.

4

General Buzz Curry

Born to be a Star!

H. A. "Buzz" Curry grew up in Oregon, the oldest of three boys in a family that moved around a lot. By the time Buzz enrolled in high school, he had attended 13 different schools. After graduating, he followed in the footsteps of an older friend who attended Southern Oregon College the prior year. Buzz liked what he heard about college life and planned to room with his pal, but on the day he was to enroll, his friend received his draft notice into the military.

In September 1966, a friend of Buzz's father gave Buzz a 300-mile lift to Ashland, Oregon to enroll in college. Buzz got out of the car with his suitcase and was left standing alone on the curb. He had little family support, so he figured out what he needed to do and applied himself.

During winter semester in his sophomore year, he carried 18 hours of courses and earned a 3.8 GPA, while working 48 hours a week on the night shift at a gas station. The following semester, things came apart, however, after his girlfriend left for a job as a flight attendant; Buzz's orbit got temporarily out of whack. By semester's end, he had failed most of his classes, dropped out of school, and, rather than wait, he volunteered for the draft into the U.S. Army in order to have some choice in military assignments. At that point, his Army career plan was simple: do his time, learn what he could, live through Vietnam, then get out and re-start his life.

Thirty-two years later, Buzz retired from the Army as a Brigadier General. Along the way, he completed his bachelor's degree in business at St. Martin's College in Washington State and also earned a master's degree in business. In addition, he completed paratrooper training and earned the Special Forces "Green Beret". He applied for and was accepted in Officer Candidate School, and was commissioned a second lieutenant Infantry in 1970. But perhaps his most significant milestone was in 1969 when a flight attendant named Laury caught a flight to Oregon and she and Buzz married in their home state. Buzz, a private first class at the time, was granted a two-week leave for the occasion and given enough money from Army Relief to finance a bare-bones honeymoon. His wife liked Army life and was a natural success as an officer's wife. In Buzz's own words, his Army career "just rolled along."

Today, a dozen years or more after retiring from the Army, Buzz has time scheduled for working on the house, boating trips, motorhome adventures, and travel. He and his wife spend time with their family, and he enjoys entertaining friends with his story-telling while cooking seafood he harvested himself. Friends often come to him looking for advice on home or boat maintenance. He listens carefully to the description of a problem, asks a few questions for clarification, then often says something like, *It sounds like a two-man job, and you're going to need a heavy-duty grinder. I happen to have a heavy-duty grinder. I think we could work together and get this thing done, so when do you want to do it?*

He's a doer. A man in motion.

So, what can we learn from the story of a young man who flamed out of college by the end of his sophomore year, became an Army enlistee with no career plans, no support from family, no money, and fresh out of options? Plenty.

Buzz said he was a very active kid, the kind who would much rather run out the door in search of friends and adventure than sit down and read a book. The kind of kid who liked to take chances, who sometimes jumped off a roof when he thought he could make it.

What did Buzz have going for him that accounts for this success? For one thing, he was always able to learn from his experiences. Buzz is thoughtful, and analyzes his experiences and results carefully.

Here are some key observations about his life and Army career:

Risk taking. As mentioned previously, Buzz was drawn to risks, like jumping off a roof. If he thought he could make it, he'd do it. However, in Buzz's mind, the value was not in being the boldest daredevil, but rather in the experience he gained in assessing risks, in making go-no-go decisions, and in building self-confidence that comes from being a successful risk taker. He believes people should be encouraged to take more risks. This doesn't mean doing dangerous stunts. You may not want to jump off a roof, wind-surf in 40 knots of breeze, or ski double black diamond slopes.

You *can* experience risk taking by volunteering for activities outside your comfort zone. If you are on a football team, consider taking a part in a theatre production, or volunteer on the stage crew. If you find church services boring, volunteer to help out with Sunday school, or find an opportunity to spend Sunday mornings reading to elderly shut-ins at an assisted living facility. Work with an entirely different group of people you may never have met otherwise. Volunteer opportunities offer rich experiences to those willing to take a risk, to try something different. Experience life outside the box and learn new lessons. Like Buzz, you can hone good judgment skills and build self-confidence by taking risks.

Leadership and leading by example. In 1985, Buzz was assigned to the position of battalion commander for the 28th Transportation Battalion in Germany. He described this as the most rewarding post of his entire career. The battalion consisted of five companies, each with approximately 150 soldiers, plus a crew of 35 to 40 officers and non-commissioned officers. Buzz was the senior officer of approximately 1,000 soldiers on this team. Both he and Laury, as a commander's wife, were expected to lead by example, and to make the experience of serving in the

28th Transportation Battalion a positive lesson for all. From the beginning, Buzz saw this as an opportunity to do things they could both be proud of for the rest of their lives, to leave a legacy and to help motivate and inspire soldiers.

Buzz believes just about anybody can become a leader to some degree. Using one of his favorite analogies, football, he said, "Anybody can learn to be a quarterback: study the plays and learn them; put on your uniform in the locker room; practice calling the signals, taking the snap, handing off or throwing a pass—we all can learn these things. But the player with greater athletic skills, with sharper reflexes, better judgment, and greater self-confidence will be the superior quarterback."

The same applies to leadership, and senior officers were always looking for junior officers who possessed the potential for superior leadership. It was an unwritten obligation, an expectation, for senior officers to seek out promising junior officers to coach and mentor. When asked how a junior officer might best present himself as a candidate for mentoring, Buzz replied, "By busting your butt, doing your job."

In my experience, this is always good advice for anyone trying to succeed.

The armed services has a very different career environment: promote from within, and up or out. What this means Is that the most brilliant and successful leaders in business or government will never be candidates for senior officer positions, for example, in the Army, unless they are willing to start as second lieutenants and earn their promotions one at a time. It also means that if you find yourself deemed non-promotable—even after ten or fifteen years of service—and are moved into less responsible positions, you are probably facing retirement within a few years at your current level. Leadership ability is a significant factor in deciding whether an officer is promotable. Officers who are judged to be 'low flyers' are shunted off to less responsible positions. They get the message and retire, or resign. This is a significant difference compared to careers in business.

Many businesses accommodate skilled, mature employees who have reached their career peak, but who continue to make contributions. They may not be promotable, but as long as the organization needs their contributions they remain on the job. The technology sector, for example, has many employees at the senior engineer or senior programmer levels with 10 to 15 years experience who are valuable contributors, but may never be promoted further because they lack leadership or management skills, or choose not to take on those roles.

As a rule of thumb, you can expect that 75% of Army officers at the captain level will earn promotions to major, and 75% of majors will be promoted to lieutenant colonel. Then the funnel becomes very narrow: 50% of lieutenant colonels will move on to full colonel, but only 1% of colonels will be promoted to brigadier general. As you can imagine, leadership ability is very much on the mind of every captain, major and colonel who plans for a successful career in the Armed Services.

Buzz said some of the most valuable mentoring was

in the informal "footlocker counseling"—when a junior officer was taken aside by a senior officer or an experienced non-commissioned officer (NCO) for off-the-cuff instruction or coaching.

One of his most powerful memories was when an NCO invited Buzz, then an enlisted man, to visit his home for dinner, meet his family, and act like a "regular" human being. Buzz says that until that event, NCOs were the guys screaming in your face, bombarding you with threats and negative messages. It was an impactful and positive revelation to him when that man thought enough of him to take him aside and open his home to a young soldier, to know him from a different perspective.

Building a Reputation. An Army officer may have 20 to 30 years on the job by the time he or she is eligible for the last one or two promotions. After spending this much time building a career, an officer has also established a reputation, documented by proficiency reports and promotion boards, and also the unwritten, but not necessarily unspoken opinions of many fellow officers one has worked with over the years. Buzz built his reputation based on the following qualities: Self-confidence. Reasonableness. Not a 'screamer'. Treated everyone with respect and dignity. Tough, yet fair. Human.

Life experience. The experience of attending 13 different schools before graduating from high school clearly had a significant impact on Buzz, and a positive one. He enjoys telling stories—well, it goes well beyond storytelling. He is gregarious. He engages strangers in conversation at a party, and he can command the attention of an audience of strangers. Beyond being sociable, Buzz is thoughtful, his words are well chosen, he doesn't try to sell you or snow you, and what he has to say is interesting and worthwhile.

When Buzz talks about his early experiences, one understands that moving to so many different environments as a kid was challenging. As he said, if you make a mistake and get involved with the wrong crowd, you have to stop, back out, change direction and then reconnect with the right crowd—none of which is easy. Dealing with those challenges gave him confidence and, like jumping off the roof, after he had done it a few times, he knew he could trust his judgment and successfully assimilate into new groups. He developed a self-confidence that stayed with him throughout his career.

He considers growing up without a lot of material success as another positive influence. Buzz definitely wanted to provide more for Laury and his family than what he experienced as a child. To do this he needed a successful career. For a junior officer, or a junior employee in any large organization who wants success and wants to provide a good life for spouse and family, the old proverb, "Necessity is the mother of invention" may translate into "Bust your butt, do a good job, become a member of a can-do team."

Whether you plan to pursue a career in the military or choose careers in other fields, there are valuable universal lessons we can all learn by examining the careers of Buzz and others.

5

Jake Culp

Communications: "Write it. Speak it."

Jake is retired and lives in a beautiful home in Maryland with his lovely wife of more than 50 years, Jill. I first met Jake and Jill when we were sophomores in high school in Bethesda, a Maryland suburb of Washington, D.C. Jake was a friendly guy in high school, very smart, and yet good natured and somewhat self- effacing. He had a good sense of humor and often told stories where the joke was on him. It didn't surprise anyone when Jake was elected senior class president at Walter Johnson High School. He had been elected class president each year beginning in junior high, and no one ran against him in his junior and senior years.

Jake attended Penn State University, where he pledged Phi Delta Theta, served as its president, and was also elected vice president of the Interfraternity Council. After four years at Penn State he graduated, married Jill, and began his career teaching high school in Pennsylvania.

Teaching high school didn't agree with him. Jake left after the first year and enrolled in graduate school at the University of Maryland. One year later, with a master's degree, he was ready to make his second start on a career. But before we dive into that story, let's take a look at Jake's experiences in school and how they helped prepare him for career success.

On the one hand, Jake was a young man in his mid-20s with not much to brag about in terms of career success. He graduated from Penn State in four years, tried teaching for a year and didn't like it. He enrolled in graduate school, earned a master's degree in two years, and was ready for a new start in a different field.

What did he have going for himself that might catch the attention of an employer? Well, quite a bit. By earning his undergraduate degree in four years, and a master's degree in two, Jake demonstrated that he could apply himself to achieve important long-term goals. His experiences in student government and college fraternity life gave him the opportunity to run a lot of meetings, lead a lot of projects, and work with a lot of people.

Jake points out that introverts usually have a difficult time being effective leaders. While in high school and college, he enjoyed, and became good at, the give and take of working with other students to plan and define projects, solve problems, and develop consensus. He enjoyed the process, and was able to lead and help organize to achieve results. Through all of his experience, he developed confidence that he could achieve important goals and work with others in a leadership role—valuable skills for anyone desiring to go into management.

Jake said one of the most valuable lessons he learned was that he saw many highly intelligent and capable colleagues who had years of career success under their belts, yet failed miserably when they were thrust into leadership positions. They were brilliant scientists or researchers, but they did not have enough leadership experience, and they lacked self-confidence in their ability to lead.

Jake's best advice for acquiring leadership skills, especially for students, is to seek volunteer opportunities that provide experiences to supplement what is introduced in a classroom. Look for leadership experience everywhere. The greatest opportunities can be found by volunteering for local organizations, or a global foundation. Your experiences as a volunteer will help unlock a lot of doors.

Master's degree accomplished, Jake decided on a new career as a Federal Government Management Intern at the National Institutes of Health (NIH) in Bethesda. The management intern program is designed to attract and train future managers for all branches of the federal government, and is just one of quite a few career programs focused on recent college graduates. (Truman Fellowships is another.) Jake thrived at NIH, and even though it has been more than 45 years since he started there, he still speaks enthusiastically about the help he received from his first two mentors.

The two experienced managers coached, trained, steered and managed Jake for five plus years until he was ready to move on to the next phase of his career. Fortunately for Jake, he chose a career path where mentoring was an integral part of the process, and that helped kick-start his career. His managers were committed to the success of the intern program, and they understood part of their job was to function as an effective mentor for Jake.

(As you meet with with potential employers, ask, "How do I learn the ropes?" The more structured a mentorship program, the more likely your first years will help put you ahead of the game.)

For 36 years, Jake was a successful federal government manager and executive, working for many agencies in administrative, executive, and policy making positions. He said his most rewarding position was serving as Deputy Director of the Office of Rural Health Policy, planning health programs and service delivery in all fifty states at a time when rural hospitals were closing and doctors were leaving smaller communities to accept positions in metropolitan health systems. In this position, he served on a committee with fifty state governors, all focused on the rural health challenge. Today, many years later, he and some of his fellow committee members convene for lunch meetings on a regular basis to maintain friendships and discuss common interests.

Jake's career in the federal government took him from his first job as an intern to significant assignments in the Senior Executive Service. During our interviews, we discussed personal elements that helped him succeed, which included willingness to take some risks and being flexible. (In his case, teaching didn't work out, so he tried something different.) He remained open to new opportunities, tried new paths, and avoided complacency or being stuck in a dead-end assignment.

In addition to experience gained from his leadership roles in high school and college, Jake identified key skills he attributes to his success:

> As for my career, the best advice I ever received was to develop writing skills. I always did well on college essay exams because I could write reasonably well. I made a point of improving on that skill and found it to be invaluable. So many of the young people I recruited into government positions had master's degrees or even better in subjects like public health administration, business administration, political science, etc., but had never learned how to write a coherent sentence or paragraph.
>
> Writing skills are important in just about any field I can imagine, especially in this age of Twitter, Facebook, and other electronic media that make it much more difficult for people to learn and practice effective writing skills.
>
> I bet that many of your respondents are going to stress the importance of public speaking skills and I would not disagree with that. However, I would also stress that people starting in their careers should

> identify bosses and colleagues who are especially effective at leading meetings, and learn from them. Leading a good meeting is a terrific skill for making the best use of time, team building, and the exercise of leadership. It is a skill that is hard to describe, but a good observer will know it when he or she sees it.

Jake makes some good points. We would probably all agree that a person with good writing skills will tend to have an easier time of it on essay tests. And if you are asking for help, or trying to persuade or advocate for a particular point of view, your text message or email will probably be more successful the better you are at writing. Having good verbal and written communications skills are important, no matter what career you choose.

6

Making Your Point

Advice on public speaking and effective professional writing

Being able to communicate effectively is probably the most valuable skill you can acquire—for both professional and personal success. You don't have to be Ernest Hemingway to be an effective writer. What you do have to have is confidence and a good editor. You don't have to be a great orator to get your point across in a meeting.

Let's pause from my contributors' stories and I'll explain what I mean. A couple of years ago I had the bad luck to be in two separate freeway accidents involving multiple cars within a six-month span. The first accident was in midtown Seattle, when I was driving home from my son's house on a grey foggy day with limited visibility. As traffic ahead slowed,

I braked to a crawl, and was suddenly rammed from the rear by a person talking on a cell phone. My vehicle needed more than $18,000 in repairs and two weeks in the collision shop before I was back in business.

Within a couple of weeks, I was driving to Seattle when traffic slowed going up a hill, then came to a stop. I was again rammed from the rear, but this time the impact drove my car into the stopped vehicle in front of me. To add insult to my injury, the traffic officer on the scene sent me a summons to appear in traffic court for excessive speed. The court was more than 50 miles from my home. I felt harassed and unjustly charged, and I needed a plan to respond to this problem. After reviewing my options described in the summons paperwork, which included a written statement in lieu of appearing in court, I decided to write a letter to the traffic court judge, explaining the circumstances.

I know I am not an exceptional writer, but I also know that, with effort, I can tell my story and make my point in an organized and persuasive way without offending the reader. If you have ever been to traffic court, you understand that I would to do almost anything rather than represent myself in front of a judge in that environment. If you had the option of telling your story in writing, and you had confidence in your ability to do just that, wouldn't that be a much more appealing option?

I wrote my account of the accident, my wife edited my work, and I sent it to the judge. The charges were dropped. This story has a happy outcome, not due to my writing skills, but due to my self-confidence that I could communicate my case effectively in writing. How did I gain this confidence? Practice. By taking courses in journalism in high school and college, despite the fact that I did not want to work as a journalist. By taking classes in creative writing. By writing short stories, none of which were ever published. By spending enough time stringing words together and subjecting my work to critical review that I developed confidence that I could, if I put some effort into it, communicate effectively in writing.

How might you develop effective skills in written communications? By writing. Take journalism or creative writing classes. Keep a journal. Start a blog. Write freelance articles for a magazine or newspaper. And read a lot. Free online publications cover just about any industry: transportation, technology, finance, marketing, foreign policy, …and writing. In addition to online resources, visit your local library. Public libraries subscribe to several trade magazines in print form.

At times, what you've written may have to be verbalized. Develop good verbal communication skills. Whether preparing for a job interview, presenting a proposal, or explaining a project before a group of your peers or management, you'll need to effectively communicate, deliver your pitch, carry on a conversation with people you don't know. Speaking before an audience, large or small, can be nerve-wracking. Be prepared, and practice.

Earlier this year, my wife and I were on a Gig Harbor Yacht Club cruise to Bremerton and, as is to be expected in the spring, it was alternately drizzling and raining on the team trying to barbeque steaks for dinner. I had been casually chatting with one of my boating pals, describing my ideas for this book and seeking feedback. He got the concept of career building skills immediately, and volunteered that the most important skill for him was the ability to speak in front of an audience. His academic career was in sciences, he explained, and like most of his peers he dreaded presenting papers and research reports. But he understood that presenting his findings, research results, and ideas was important, a skill in itself that would complement his scientific work. He decided to become good at public speaking, and he worked at it until he accomplished his goal. In the meantime, his career advanced and he wound up running a statewide utility company, retired, and now enjoys sailing his lovely sailboat any day the wind is blowing over Puget Sound.

Of course, it isn't as easy as simply deciding that you want to become good at public speaking. Let me describe another recent experience my wife, Sarah, and I shared. We were recruited to be judges at Senior Day at our local high school, the day when each senior student delivers a stand-up report on his or her senior project.Sarah and I were on different judging panels, so we each heard seven or eight different students describe their projects.There were some extremely smart, talented students presenting, and the projects were often amazing.One self-described math nerd organized a math tutoring project at the local Boys and Girls Club, where younger kids congregated every day after school. Another student put together a Christmas party for kids in Tijuana, and raised the money to buy the presents and transport her team to Mexico to deliver them.

Their reports included PowerPoint presentations, and each student stood at a lectern, facing the audience of half a dozen judges and an equal number of fellow students. The PowerPoint slides ranged from fair to sensationally good, but their delivery—the public speaking—was poor: there just isn't any other way to describe it.The students stood rigidly at the lectern, spoke inaudibly or without emphasis or inflection, spent too much time looking at their notes or the projector screen, and seemed to be afraid to try to engage their audience. I asked one presenter to describe how he prepared for the big day, and he said he had read his presentation to his dog—once. I asked one of the teachers on the panel how many of the graduating seniors had taken a class in public speaking, and she explained that there was no class in public speaking, per se, but they were able to include public speaking instruction in many of the other classes. Well, it was clear that this isn't working. Speaking in front of an audience is such a daunting challenge for many of us that we must work hard at getting good at it.

This is such a valuable skill, I recommend that every student take a speech class or join the debate team in high school. If this isn't possible, look for classes offered at community colleges or adult education facilities. Consider joining Toastmasters International: they have an interesting website which describes their educational purpose and the operation of nearly 14,000 clubs in 129 countries around the world. A quick locator search using my home zip code turned up 16 clubs within ten miles.

One of the reasons speaking in front of an audience can be so frightening is that most of us don't have to do it very often. Unless you are a pastor or an actor, you don't find yourself addressing an audience of strangers every week. At one point in my career, I was responsible for worldwide technical support for all Micom Systems communications products. We had hundreds of thousands of modems and multiplexors installed supporting HP, DEC and other minicomputer installations, and when communications networks didn't work quite right, our end users and our international distributors would call our tech support team in California for help.

Every year we hosted a conference for our international distributors, and every year I would be expected to speak at the conference about our plans for enhancing technical support. One year, the conference was scheduled for the Universal Studios in Los Angeles and a large crowd was expected. The presentations would be in the main ballroom, with a raised stage, an enormous screen behind the podium, and sophisticated lights and sound. It was a Hollywood production, but I was not a movie star. I was scared silly. The fact that I had survived a presentation to this group a year earlier did not make me at all confident. But I was able to make that presentation without embarrassing myself, and even earned some compliments. Let me tell you how I did it: hard work and practice.

It wasn't difficult to write the presentation and lay out the PowerPoint slides. We had a team helping prepare slides using a standard corporate format, so I knew that the materials projected on the screen behind me would look professional, and my speech would make sense–if I could just get it out. I thought more than once that it would be a blessing for all concerned if I could just mail each attendee a copy of my remarks; but the reality was that I was going to climb up the steps to that stage and the audience expected a confident and coherent description of the technical support we were planning for the coming year.

So you could say that what I was grappling with was the presentation itself, the act of standing up in front of that crowd and explaining my plans, making a positive impression, coming across like the executive and business partner I was paid to be. I was still scared.

I attacked the problem by practicing. I practiced my speech until I knew it cold. I could recite it in the shower. Then, in the set-up days before the start of the conference, I spent time in the ballroom. I practiced climbing the stairs to the stage and walking to the podium. I carried a folder with my notes and practiced arranging it on the podium. I had the audio/visual team adjust the lights as they would be when I was speaking, and am I ever glad I did this.

Standing at that podium, looking out at the audience, all I could see was blackness. The house lights were dimmed so the projected slides would be crisp and in sharp focus on the screen behind me. Looking out was like looking into deep space but without the stars, or looking down a well. There was no connection with the audience whatsoever. So in addition to getting a feel for the stage and the choreography of walking to and from the lectern, I also added a few jokes to my speech in order to get some audible feedback from the folks I was addressing.

I must have visited the ballroom and climbed onto the stage six or seven times before it was my turn to speak. When the meeting adjourned for lunch or a coffee break, I stayed behind and practiced, not reciting my remarks, just getting familiar with the space. It was a lot like a baseball team warming up before the game: after you field a few balls and make a few throws to first base you get used to the playing field.

It sounds simple, perhaps even simple-minded, to stress the need to practice. However, if you think about it, what do star athletes do between games and before Super Bowls, World Series, and major tournaments?

They practice!

7

Helen Stewart

A Strong Woman

Helen Stewart lives with her husband, Alan, in a large home in the Pacific Northwest with walls of southwest-facing windows looking out over the Puget Sound and the Olympic mountain range. Helen works daily at her career as a financial advisor with Morgan Stanley, and Alan is a retired director of operations of an Oregon utility company.

They enjoy their sailboat, and Helen also owns a riding horse and competes in dressage events. (She began riding seriously while in college.) In dressage, the horse and rider communicate closely with each other. It's a discipline that requires balance, strength, flexibility and precision. Helen pointed out that equestrian events are one of the few sports in which men and women compete in the same events on an equal basis, including in the Olympic Games.

Somewhere around age 14, Helen decided she wanted to pursue a career in business and finance, and after graduation from Santa Monica High School, she went on to earn a Bachelor of Arts in Economics at UC Davis. Her parents encouraged her to develop a strong work ethic and expected her to work at responsible summer jobs, beginning at age 16. She worked in banks and enjoyed the work. She took six months off from college and worked at United California Bank in Santa Monica. By the time she finished college, she had worked at three or four banks.

Early in her high school years, her parents took her to France for an extended visit and enrolled her in a French public school, where she had to scramble to keep up and absorb instruction in a second language. She found that this experience helped build confidence in herself.

After college, Helen returned to Los Angeles and a job as a financial analyst with a mortgage investment company. Her next employer was the trust and investment department of an asset management group as a research assistant. When she attended analysts meetings, she was always one of few female analysts in the room. Nevertheless, she began thinking about a career in investing, rather than banking.

I asked Helen how she developed the self-confidence necessary to pursue a career in a field so dominated by men. She responded that growing up with four older brothers and many strong female role models helped her to develop expectations for herself, and gain the self-confidence necessary to set goals and achieve them. She also learned a few important lessons about goals and teamwork through her membership in a Brownie troop, and then as a Girl Scout until age 18. Her mother, a Christian Scientist, introduced her to the works of Mary Baker Eddy, which became an important influence in her life. Helen said that her faith and a belief that things would work out for the best gave her strength to pursue her career goals.

One of Helen's managers at the asset management firm suggested she look into the Chartered Financial Analyst (CFA) program, a professional qualification for college graduates working in finance, particularly in investing, that many considered as valuable a credential as an MBA. Earning the CFA designation is a tough go: a college degree, four years of experience in finance, plus three years of self-study and preparation for three difficult, six-hour exams. The exams are no joke. Each year, half or more of the candidates sitting for the exams will not pass.

Helen committed to earning the CFA designation, began studying, and found that she enjoyed learning the details of the investment business. In some ways it must have seemed like learning dressage: she was preparing for three big events—the three CFA exams where she would be one of a very few women taking an exam, competing with men on a level playing field with her brains, determination, and confidence in herself.

After three years, Helen had her CFA—just in time to learn that her husband was walking out. She needed a stable and good-paying career to support herself and her young son.

The next major stop on her career path was joining a nine-employee investment management firm, Morley Financial, in Portland, Oregon, where she soon became the credit manager. Her job was to analyze risks and potential rewards of investing in various companies, including life insurance companies, including Executive Life of California, the largest life insurance company in that state in the mid-1980s. Helen was asked to conduct a review of their operations and investment potential, and she turned them down. She didn't like their massive investments in high-yield junk bonds or their reliance on a single line of business.

By turning thumbs down on the deal, Helen pitted herself against some big guns in the industry: Fred Carr, the CEO of Executive Life and his business associate Michael Milken, chief of the high-yield bond department at Drexel, Burnham. And she was right. Within a couple of years, Executive Life was insolvent, the biggest insurance company failure the world had yet seen. Milken headed for jail and Drexel pleaded guilty to federal charges.

Helen stayed at Morley Financial for 16 years, and the founder, Hal Morley, became a key mentor. She continued to focus on her professional development, and wrote an article that was published in Pension World, an industry publication. While at Morley, she met and married Alan, who shared her love of horses, sailing and dancing. Life was good. Work was good.

In 2002, Russell Investments in Washington State recruited her for Director of Credit Research. This was a major career step up and included serving as the chair of the investment committee, a group of 15 executives. Helen said, "For a while it didn't even cross my mind that I was the only woman because I was so used to working with men."

Alan was still working in Portland, so Helen settled into her new job and lived on their sailboat during the week. After a couple of years, she and Alan bought a home in a small community nearby. But this was not to be the final chapter in her career. The financial crisis hit and put an end to her job with Russell Investments—just after Alan retired and joined Helen in Washington, and as they were renovating their new home.

Helen regrouped and began building her practice as a financial advisor with Morgan Stanley. Now in her seventh year, she has a growing list of clients. She enjoys working with them, and she also enjoyed working with her son, Joseph, who graduated from U.C. Berkeley with a degree in economics and shared Helen's practice for three years before moving to Portland.

Helen has served on the board of Girl Scouts of Western Washington, a $15 million non-profit supporting 26,000 Girl Scouts. She also followed a tradition of the women of her family by being an active member of a church, where she serves as a Sunday School teacher. She and Alan travel frequently, most recently on a cruise around Cape Horn.

She earned her career success, enjoys a good life, and offers the following advice:

> Choose strong role models. For me, as a woman, it has been the strong women in my life. My mother

> was a Wellesley graduate. My aunt graduated from Radcliffe. One of my father's female cousins had a law degree, and was in charge of liquidating a bank during the Great Depression. Many of the women in my family were strong women.
>
> These strong role models really built my confidence. Over the past year or so, I have been thinking about confidence a lot and how important a factor it is. If you don't have confidence then you don't try things, or you give up when things are difficult. Persistence is key.
>
> Success is not about whether or not you fall; it's about how you get up again.

Additional thoughts Helen shared from her experience:

Be coachable. Take action on suggestions that are given to you, such as earning a professional certification; as in Helen's case, Chartered Financial Analyst (CFA) or Certified Public Accountant (CPA).

Build confidence. Don't waste time and effort worrying about failure. Concentrate on strengths; and strengthen weaknesses.

Work smart and lead a balanced life. Helen emphasized that she never worked 60-hour weeks. Becoming successful doesn't mean sacrificing all of your personal time.

In final thoughts, times have changed. Look at all the woman CEOs in business today. Helen believes that women have broken the glass ceiling and are competing on a much more equal basis in the workplace. Like dressage, it's how you perform that counts, and gender doesn't enter into it. What matters is your ability, your hard work and preparation, and your confidence on the field. Helen is a winner—on her horse, in the executive suite, or helping her clients prepare for retirement. She will have a very happy day when she joins her husband in retirement and enjoys the fruits of their labor.

8

Bob Berman

Luck, Cards, and Hustle

Warren Buffet said his success is mainly due to good luck: he was lucky to be born a male at a time when most of the work force was male. He was lucky to be born in the United States, where, in addition to offering opportunities to succeed, he was able to obtain a good education, medical care, and plenty of solid Midwestern food, including his favorite—cheeseburgers and steaks. In addition to being one of the world's most successful investors, Buffett also stands out as one of the smartest, shrewdest businessmen of the past 50 years.

I have read with great enjoyment every book I could find by or about Warren Buffet, and I recommend that anyone who wants to achieve success, in any field, to do the same.

Most folks preparing to be successful may not have much in common with Buffet. Some of you may be at a point in your life where you definitely do not feel lucky—where you are sitting at the card table with another bad hand—and you feel about as far from success as you are from joining the Billionaire's Club.

One of the smartest business executives I ever met is Kirk Matthews, co-founder and chairman of Xircom, a successful California technology company where I worked for several years in the 1990s. Matthews assembled an officer team he referred to as his "phony-baloney executives" and we were focused on achieving his vision of a successful, fast-growing, profitable technology company which would quickly go public and make us all rich. He was a pragmatist; however, he would not tolerate any lapses in performance, judgment or behavior that threatened company goals. He explained that you need to be clear in your own mind about what game you are playing. His position was that he was playing bridge and making the best hand out of the cards dealt—to play the cards skillfully, make the most of the hand that he held. Playing poker, you might choose to bluff, if dealt a poor hand; but in most cases you would throw in your cards, fold your hand, save your money and wait for a winning hand.

Working for Matthews at Xircom, one had a sense that we were all working together to achieve clear objectives, which were important to each of us as individuals. Although several executives left the team because of conflicts or performance issues, most of us believed we would be on the team that collected the rewards so long as we paid attention to the hands we were dealt and played them as best we could. And that turned out to be the case.

Bob Berman, one of my high school classmates, turned a badly dealt hand into a highly successful career at a prestigious investment firm. Bob's career success should be an inspiration to anyone who thinks the odds are against them.

At the age of 61, Bob Berman retired from Raymond James Financial, where he had enjoyed a successful career as a top-producing financial planner. Although Raymond James was recognized as both an outstanding place to work and a prestigious investment firm, Bob wanted more free time to spend with his wife of 30 years, Donna, who was fighting cancer. Bob also wanted time for the rest of his family, which included their children, and Bob's father, who was in his early 90s.

Bob was financially well-off, and counted on his investments to add to his wealth in retirement. You might think that Bob was probably a finance major in college, perhaps with an MBA or CPA. But he wasn't. Bob earned an associate degree after two years at a junior college. But life dealt him a weak hand and he was not in a position to earn a four-year degree. At age 20, Bob was unemployed, married, and soon to become a father, with no job prospects or career plans.

Bob described the situation.

> Needless to say, any plans I had were seriously altered. I was thrown into the rude world of work—real work, no kidding around work—and attended

> George Washington University at night. Meanwhile, I got divorced, was nearly drafted into the military, and got into advertising sales at the Washington Evening Star newspaper.

He did not have many options. A young man with no degree or work experience or family business was probably smart to go into selling, as long as it seemed a good fit. For Bob it was an excellent fit. He had always been very social, and had a strong sense of curiosity which prompted him to ask lots of questions—an excellent tactic for a salesman. In addition, strong verbal skills were developed at the dinner table by discussing history, politics, and current events with his intellectual parents. And necessity was giving him a big push. He needed a job for two simple reasons: the money, and the need to become a success.

When Bob and I were growing up, kids in our neighborhood played baseball all summer on Little League and junior league teams. Bob and I were sometimes on the same team and in most ways he was the superior baseball player. Quite a mix of kids were on each team; some were standout athletes and other were not athletically gifted. Despite the fact that we were never on a team of all-stars, winning was important and we would yell and cheer every success in every game, reaching for inspiration even if our team was outgunned. The highest compliment was given when a teammate deserved an accolade, gave his all on a play. We'd yell out, "Way to hustle!" It was a reward for an obvious display of determination, of trying your absolute hardest to catch a hard ground ball, or a running catch in the outfield, beating out a throw to first base or stealing second. Even an overweight, slow kid could earn a compliment for hustle if they tried their best and succeeded.To hustle meant that you clearly and obviously did your utmost to help win the game for your team. Bob earned a lot of "way to hustle" call-outs in Little League. He learned the value of hustle when he decided to get into the sales game ten years later.

Working for the Evening Star, Bob learned a few important facts very quickly. First, he was well qualified. The recruiter didn't ask about college or degrees—he was looking for young men who wanted to make money in sales. The second thing Bob learned was there were no older, experienced salespeople at the Star. They were all young men trying to figure out how to make money and become successful, all pretty much in the same boat.

Training was minimal, so they had to learn the ropes on their own. Bob's advice:

> Mentors were the key. I did well and made good friends with other young guys trying to make it. 'Trying to make it' included sharing ideas and making them work. It was really helpful; not one mentor, but four or five.

Many mornings the sales team left the Star offices and rendezvoused at a coffee shop nearby for a brainstorming session. It worked. Bob became successful and was on his way.

Bob spent a couple of years at the Star, then a couple of more at a small newspaper in Arlington, Virginia where he did everything but set type, learning the print media business. Then he discovered WOL-Soul, an R&B station located in Washington, D.C. He loved it! Once again, Bob was selling ads, but this time the sales manager became an extremely effective mentor. Bob said he learned what it was like not only to sell ads, but also to collect money and write ads.

> He was a tough taskmaster, but I was having such a good time, I could not tell. He later was in my wedding to Donna in 1969. Again, a mentor was instrumental in getting me on the right road.
>
> I learned a very valuable lesson during this entire period, but did not realize it until much later on: the last person you want to fool is yourself. You know when you aren't trying hard enough.

Bob was also learning the value of hard work—hustle—in achieving career success. Bob and Donna left WOL-Soul to move to St. Petersburg, Florida, to join Donna's father in his baby furniture business. The industry was changing, and the business was falling behind. Bob spent a rough ten years working for his father-in-law, but he learned a lot:

> I worked in the factory during the day, and ran a sales crew and made sales calls at night. I devised a letter to be sent to expectant mothers that was mailed on Saturdays, and by Monday we had

> enough appointments to get us through the week. It was a about a thirty percent response. While it was a rough experience and tough on us, because this was not how it was supposed to be, I have to hand it to my father-in-law because he showed me how to prospect.
>
> I could be dropped in a city anywhere and develop leads just talking to people. I was on the road, training new distributors and making sales in the middle of nowhere to prove it could be done. I wrote and produced a training film to make the job easier, but I still was in the field under pressure of making a sale. Making that film brought me back to the days at the newspapers and radio station when I created and sold ads, so I knew I had some creative ability.

Once again, Bob's boss, in this case his father-in-law, became an effective mentor, and Bob also stepped into the mentor role himself, running a sales crew and recruiting and training distributors in other parts of the country.

The baby furniture business was not healthy and Bob had to make a change. He investigated a tax shelter sales opportunity, but the more he dug into the details, the more concerned he became.

> Not comfortable, I sought out Donna's friend's husband, Tom James, chairman of a small St. Petersburg brokerage firm, now named Raymond

> James Financial (RJF). I wanted to know if this tax shelter was a security and what he thought of the deal in general. He made his comments and then said that if I was going to sell, to work for him.
>
> I had no money, never owned a stock or a bond and told him so, but he insisted that I think about it.

Within six months, Bob left the furniture business and started as the first trainee at Raymond James Financial. He was 38 years old.

RJF recruited more trainees, and Bob found a lot in common with his peers. They were in their 30s and 40s, career changers looking for success, and they had come up through the school of hard knocks, like he did. In February 1981, he was the only RJF trainee who took the required Series 7 exam, or General Securities Representative Exam.

> My experience with the furniture business left me exhausted, so working at a real company—even starting with nothing—was like a vacation to me. Like most sales jobs, it took at least two years to catch any traction, but in the meantime I found that I was a natural at the investment business.
>
> I soaked up everything I came in touch with and my sense of curiosity put me in good stead as I began to understand how investments were structured. Investments fascinated me, but my background in selling is what made the difference. In the early 1980s, no one was doing well, but since I was

new and had no real clients, I had no idea business was bad. I thought it was a good thing that interest rates rose every day.

Most of the people I met were more or less in the same situation, so we clung together like survivors on a life raft. We talked all the time and met on Fridays for dinner. It was then that I really learned what I needed to know. The key person in the group, a man named Phil, became a very good friend. He was an experienced broker and counseled me. We spoke every day for over twenty years.

I rose rapidly in the firm and for over fifteen years was in the top ten of brokers in terms of production and assets under management. Phil died a tragic death a three years ago, but we remain friends with his wife and family to this day.

As a financial planner, Bob called on his years of sales and marketing experience to develop innovative strategies for finding prospects. He offered a seminar for what one needs to know about Required Minimum Distributions (RMDs) from your IRAs, 401(k) plans, etc. He discovered that very few retirees understood the rules for RMDs, and by offering this service he was able to fill his seminar seats with prospects.

When Donna was diagnosed with cancer, Bob had developed into a top producer at RJF, a successful financial advisor with an enviable book of business. He originally chose a sales career because he didn't see other, better choices. You could say he was desperate; but through his own abilities, by working hard and taking advantage of the help of others, he was successful.

After interviewing Bob at length and studying some autobiographical notes he sent me, I think I can sum up the skills, talents and personal traits that made his success possible:

» Bob worked well with mentors. He had a lot to learn, and appreciated their help.

» He understood that hard work was necessary for success, and was expected by his superiors.

» At Raymond James, he found something he wanted, something he loved to do. He knew at age 20 he was not going to become a doctor or dentist or lawyer or engineer. At Raymond James he discovered he could become a successful investment advisor and financial planner and pursue a respected profession.

» Bob is a likable guy, friendly and non-threatening. He was eager to learn. His curiosity, combined with his verbal skills, gave him important tools as a salesman.

Bob deserves a lot of credit for his success. He started his career with modest academic credentials, little sense of direction, and minimal guidance from his family. He says that after high school, all his peers went right (headed off to college) and he went left, to look for a job, search for the right career. He may have been dealt a weak hand, but he knew how to learn, he worked hard, and he knew how to hustle. The lack of choices didn't bother Bob. He chose a career in sales because it was one of few opportunities available. He played bridge and he played his hand well.

Exploring a career in sales. You may want to consider a career in sales for several reasons. Maybe the cards in your hand look a lot like Bob's, and you feel you don't have many options. Perhaps you like the fact that sales jobs are always available, anywhere in the country. Or the freedom of a sales career could be attractive to you.

To learn if sales is a fit for you, try it out. Find a part-time or summer job selling something. But make sure your production is measured and compared to peers. Just like there is no point to play golf if you don't keep score, you won't learn much about your sales aptitude if your results aren't measured and ranked with the other salespersons.

9

Aryna Swope

From Queens to Utopia

Aryna Swope grew up in Queens, New York, and graduated from high school in a class of 1,200 seniors. She was not yet 21 years old when she graduated from Simmons College in Boston, awarded Highest Distinction in a class of 300, with a degree in math and several career options ahead of her. The year was 1966 and the state of New York was facing a teacher shortage, so they offered several tempting incentives for college graduates willing to become teachers.

Aryna wasn't convinced that teaching was the best choice for her. For one thing, going into teaching was the easy, safe choice for a woman during that time, and Aryna wanted to explore other options. Graduate school was one, but she was ready and eager to earn her own living and enjoy the independence and benefits that come with a successful career. Working with the placement office at college, she arranged interviews with two platinum-level employers—Bell Labs in New Jersey, and an IBM branch office in Manhattan. Both made an offer, and she chose to sign on as a systems engineer with IBM.

In those days, IBM was preparing to launch the System 360 family of computers—the first system "family" that allowed users to start with a low-end model and, as their needs grew, move up to higher capacity models without rewriting the application software developed for the first machine. All System 360 models used the same operating systems, which was a major step forward in computing. It seems obvious today that customers would want a family of compatible computers offering different performance levels and capacities, but it was revolutionary in the early 1960s.

Fortune magazine described the development of the System 360 family—a $5 billion project—as the most expensive private development effort in the history of business, and also one of the riskiest. It paid off and by 1966, IBM was ready to ship their new 360 machines to customers in a growing worldwide market for computers.

IBM's plan was to encourage current customers to convert from their existing IBM computers to the new System 360 family, and also to sell System 360s to the thousands of prospects who had never used a computer. To accomplish these goals, they needed systems engineers—technical specialists who were trained to make technical presentations explaining computer topics, teach programming classes, and help customers design and install computers to enhance their operations. Systems engineers worked out of a sales branch office, but they were not sales people. They didn't have a sales quota and they didn't earn commissions based on sales they assisted with. They were technical specialists, valued for their knowledge and technical skills, and were paid a straight salary.

These were skills and knowledge that Aryna did not learn in school. This was before personal computers and smart phones, before Internet, before schools began offering classes in information technology. But Aryna knew that IBM would train her, and they did. Her first experience with IBM training was during her first nine weeks on the job at the IBM Regional Training Center where she studied programming languages and practiced making technical presentations.

Standing in front of an audience, making a flip-chart presentation on a technical topic was hard. She recalls her knees shaking and being unable to speak at first. She said it was a lot like learning to use a parachute: you're up in the airplane, you have the chute on, you're moving toward the door and you know what you are supposed to do, but you are so frightened you don't know whether you will be able to do it.

As it turns out, almost everyone has the same fears, and needs the same support and training to overcome them and learn new skills. The training and skill-building Aryna received helped jumpstart her career.

Initial training completed, Aryna began working as a systems engineer in a branch office. She liked the work from the start. After one year on the job, Aryna went back to the IBM training center for another six weeks of technical training. This included making technical presentations, which helped build presentation skills and confidence.

"The job was fun," she said. "I enjoyed leaving the office to visit my assigned accounts, talking with my customers, conducting training classes, making presentations, and delivering technical publications and manuals." Some 50 years later, she says this early training helped her to become confident and mature in the business world.

An IBM branch office typically housed 100 to 200 employees, divided by function: systems engineers, sales representatives, management, and administration. It didn't take Aryna long to learn that the sales reps were the most highly paid, with their commissions and bonuses on top of a base salary. In addition, they were the stars. Branch office meetings showcased the top sales people, and each year sales reps could earn recognition trips to the IBM 100% Club or the more elite Golden Circle.

Aryna began to think about switching from systems engineer to sales. Friends encouraged her ambition, and before long she talked with her manager about making the change. In other words, she raised her hand, explained what she wanted, and initiated a career change.

There were risks. Sales jobs were, and are, fundamentally different from the technical support roles of systems engineers. Sales reps were responsible for customer relationships, and reps earned commissions when customers ordered equipment. Almost all computers were rented to customers by IBM at that time, and if customers sent their

IBM equipment back, the salesman was penalized with a negative commission chargeback. Although there was no limit or cap to sales earnings, base pay for a commissioned rep was usually somewhere between 20% to 50% less than they would earn in a non-commissioned job. Reps were expected to make up the shortfall—and then some—with the commissions and bonuses they earned from their sales.

In addition to financial risks of working on commission, Aryna risked advancement in her career. Each sales rep had a quota, or responsibility for a portion of a sales team's quota. An achievement of 100% or more of your quota earned a good income and membership in the 100% Club. If the quota was not made in a year, your income suffered and your status became uncertain. You may not be reassigned or terminated, but opportunities for promotion and your eligibility for good assignments were placed on hold. Reps who did not make their numbers during their first year and continued to struggle in the second, often found some other line of work, at IBM or elsewhere, before the end of the second year. This is generally true in any sales team environment.

In IBM, there was constant public measurement and ranking of the sales reps. When you were doing well it was wonderful; but if you weren't, it could be a very negative experience.

These were the risks Aryna faced as she transitioned from systems engineer into sales. She was ready to get started and was determined to succeed. She wasn't afraid to put herself out there, and she knew how and when to ask for what she wanted. She had good managers who were encouraging mentors. She learned that she could build confidence by going out and just doing it.

Aryna's best advice:

> Don't be afraid to try. Be undeterred by the possibility of failure. Learn to accept rejection—you're in sales, remember?

Aryna did well in sales. She worked hard and she was good at relating to her customers. She also enjoyed working in a team environment and earned the trust and confidence of her managers. Before long, she moved into leadership roles and eventually was promoted to senior sales representative, and became a team leader for an IBM group focused on movie studios in Los Angeles—a very responsible position. She led her team to an important strategic victory—winning the Disney Studios account away from a rival computer company.

Asked to think about the early experiences that helped prepare her for successful leadership roles, Aryna points to her election to president of her high school sorority and the confidence she gained from her academic success; and landing a good job with a prestige employer with coaching and the support of managers.

One word Aryna used most often when discussing her career was *confidence*.

Aryna enjoys retirement and her 25-year marriage to Phil Caruthers, whose story is found in a later chapter. They live in California in the foothills of the coastal mountains—her

Utopia. Aryna describes their community as "rural, artsy, sophisticated and beautiful." They both enjoyed their 70th birthdays, and hopefully will enjoy many more.

Some of the things we can learn from Aryna's story:

- She was independent and wanted a successful career.

- She needed to find her own way. No models within her family experience guided her career choices.

- She was willing to work hard in high school and college to prepare well for the future and to build confidence.

- She was willing to be out front and knew how to raise her hand and ask for what she wanted.

- She took good care of her customers.

- She developed leadership strengths, and was well-liked as a leader.

Aryna found her Utopia by making the decision to work hard, asking for help when needed and learning from her mentors, and giving 100%.

10

Derek Kilmer

U. S. Representative

Washington's 6th Congressional District

Don't focus on what you want to be;

focus on what you want to do.

Port Angeles sits on the northwestern rim of the United States. Head west, and you can drive beside the Strait of Juan de Fuca for about 50 scenic, but lonely miles until you reach Cape Flattery—the westernmost point in the state of Washington—and the Pacific Ocean.

Port Angeles was the site of one of the largest Native American settlements, with artifacts and remains dating back 2,700 years. Today it is a city of nearly 20,000 residents, and home to Peninsula Community College and the

Peninsula Chamber of Commerce, which serve the entire Olympic Peninsula.

U.S. Representative Derek Kilmer was born in "PA", as the locals call it, the son of teachers in community schools. Growing up, Derek enjoyed playing soccer, tennis, and basketball, and playing the string bass in an orchestra and jazz band.

Timber was one of the leading industries in the Northwest, but the timber business suffered a significant decline while Derek was growing up. Troubles in the softwood/plywood industries affected all of the Northwest, but really hit hard in a remote community like Port Angeles because it is so far removed from larger towns and cities that offer employment. Lose a job in Port Angeles and you would either have to move to a larger community, such as Tacoma or Seattle, or cross your fingers and hope for an improvement in the job market before unemployment benefits ran out.

In college, Derek was interested in economics, economic development, and public policy, so that he might learn skills that would help struggling regions like the Olympic Peninsula. He found a program at Princeton University that he liked and decided to go for it. He was accepted, and with the help of scholarships, student loans, and much support from his community, he was able to attend and graduated with a Bachelor of Arts in Public Affairs.

While searching for a graduate school to work on a master's degree, Derek discovered the Marshall Scholarships, created by the British government after World War II to enable future leaders from the United States to become graduate students at leading British universities. He applied and was accepted, and three years later completed his studies for a PhD in social policy from the University of Oxford.

When I interviewed Derek, I asked what was his Plan B if the Marshall scholarship had not worked out. His answer was interesting—his educational and professional career had been more improvisational than planned. He explained that his intention was to attend graduate school to study economic development and public policy, and if the Marshall Scholarship was not available, he would have searched for another graduate school opportunity. Later I decided that this answer may well be connected to another point he made when talking about his father. His dad will soon retire after 50 years of teaching.

Derek speaks of his dad as a person who loved teaching, enjoyed a career doing something he was passionate about. He took his dad's experience to heart in his own career, and frequently recommends for people to do what they love:

> *Figure out what you want to do. Life's too short to spend years doing something that doesn't fulfill you.*

One thing is clear from Derek's career: he invested his time and energies to experience several different career opportunities. While at Princeton, he served a summer internship with the New Jersey Department of Environmental Protection, one of several environmental groups that employed him. He was also an intern with Washington's Representative Al Swift, who served eight terms in congress. Derek was an intern at the White House in 1995. All in all, he invested his talent and a lot of time looking for a career that would be as satisfying for him as his father's career was to him as a teacher.

And along the way, completely by accident, he found Jennifer, his partner, wife and mother of their children, as well as his strongest supporter. When Derek boarded a flight for London to begin his graduate school program at Oxford, he was pleased to be seated next to an attractive young woman, Jennifer. She, too, was headed for Oxford, and she was also a Marshall Scholar. Five years later, they became husband and wife.

After three years at Oxford, Derek completed studies for his PhD. He began his professional career at McKinsey & Company, a highly regarded consulting firm with clients from business, non-profits, and governments. He moved back to Washington and put his education and preparation to good use, working with and helping local clients.

McKinsey & Company is a well-known international consulting firm with more than 1,200 partners and 105 offices around the world. They recruit college graduates, MBAs, PhDs, law school graduates, and physicians, as well as experienced professionals. Applicants spend years in academia earning advanced degrees, and then look for a job at McKinsey to provide real-world experience—a chance to develop and polish leadership and problem-solving skills. McKinsey is highly selective and also has a reputation for paying well, so it is considered a good place to work and start paying off student loans.

Derek worked at McKinsey for three years, He participated in several consulting projects, primarily with clients in his own backyard in Western Washington. The next step was a ten-year stint with the Economic Development Board of Tacoma-Pierce County, where he focused on retaining jobs and attracting new employers to the region.

In 2004, Derek was elected to the Washington State House of Representatives. In 2006, he was elected to the state Senate, where he served until 2012, the year he was elected to his first term in the U.S. Congress, representing Washington's 6th Congressional District. He was elected to a second term in 2014.

Derek frequently talks about the dysfunctional nature of Congress, and is often asked whether he finds it frustrating. Following his 2014 election, he addressed the graduating class at Peninsula College in his hometown.

> This town has seen some tough times. That's what got me into economic development and then to public service because I saw the challenges. But the key for this town has not been to throw our hands up in the air and give up. Rather, we keep battling to try to turn this around.
>
> I'll tell you, I get this as a new member of Congress. People keep asking me, "Are you super frustrated?" The fact is, I'm not. Though Congress is absolutely a fixer-upper. I've decided that getting

> frustrated isn't a good use of my mental energies. It's not worthwhile to wring our hands and shake our fists at the sky when things aren't going our way.
>
> Listen, life throws all sorts of things at us. But the thing I learned growing up here is that the key is to keep moving forward. Don't get frustrated. Get motivated.

The title of this chapter focuses on one of Derek's main themes: the importance of figuring out what you want to do; what you will enjoy doing, rather than what you want to be.

Derek made very significant investments in education, and he volunteered for several significant intern positions. His first career job with McKinsey gave him exposure to multiple clients, and he had the benefit of leadership and problem-solving training from that company. Today, he seems challenged and engaged as a member of Congress, but my impression is that he might be just as fulfilled in other roles, in or out of public service, so long as he could use his economic development training and experience to do some things of significance and value.

In terms of what you take away from examining Derek's history and his advice, let me suggest that you forget that he earned a PhD at Oxford, attended an Ivy League college, and was elected to Congress. Had things turned out differently, if he had attended a community college rather than Princeton, my belief is that Derek would have had the same focus—to figure out what he wanted to do, what he wanted to accomplish in his career. I could imagine him continuing on from a community college to finish up with a four-year degree at the University of Washington, for example. I could imagine him volunteering for internships during the summers, and finding a different graduate school to pursue an advanced degree. If luck had run the other way for Derek, it is still easy to imagine him finding a way to enjoy a successful career doing what he can to make his community stronger, and a better place to live.

There's only one representative from Washington's 6th Congressional District, but there are many opportunities to do significant things for your community, state, and nation if you are willing to prepare, take risks and work hard.

Following is an excerpt from a speech Derek gave in November 2014, just days after his election to a second term in Congress. The audience was 20 young business leaders from the Kitsap Peninsula in Washington State who were being recognized for their achievements.

> As many of you know, I'm an economic development guy. Since a lot of you are young business leaders, I thought it best to give you some sound investment advice. This is it. My patented, time-tested and Kilmer approved *Top Five Pieces of Investment Advice.*

Number 5: Invest in your professional development

> Two and a half centuries ago, Benjamin Franklin wrote in his Poor Richard's Almanac, "An investment in knowledge pays the greatest interest." Even in our day and age I'm confident he still has it right. We are

living in a competitive global economy. One where we've seen a nuclear arms race replaced by a brain race. Where will the next great technological boom happen? It's safe to say that these days the United States has some competition to take that crown.

A study released in 2012 by the Organisation for Economic Cooperation and Development (OECD—I swear they are much more interesting than their name) found some startling things. By 2020, 29% of all higher education graduates aged 25-34 will get their diplomas in China. In India that number is 12% in 2020. What about the United States? 11%.

There's an old saying that change is inevitable but progress is optional. The one sure way to make forward progress in this economy is to continue to enhance your skills and marketability. That's a long way of saying, we still got this!

Look at all the great work you are doing! You are all models for what Kitsap can accomplish. You are moving our country forward. Don't forget the history of the United States. We do great things. We invest in our future. When we see the need for more students versed in fields like mathematics and science we don't get depressed, we get to work.

Investments taxpayers make in Washington State on education—whether K-12 or higher education—pay off in the long run. They help us win this new global race. And investments you make in your professional development will make sure this isn't the last award you receive.

Number 4: Invest in talking to strangers

I'm sure some of you have already struck up some interesting conversations tonight with someone you didn't know before. A wiser person than me once said there's no such thing as strangers—only friends you haven't met. I've learned a lot—and gained a lot—simply from talking to folks I don't know. I'll always have a warm spot in my heart for the fine folks of United Airlines because of a stranger I met on one of their planes.

Though it's hard to imagine, I actually met my wife, Jennifer, when I sat next to her on a flight across the Atlantic Ocean. We struck up a conversation and hit it off (even choosing to bypass most of the in-flight movie). Five years later we were married. But I've gained more than a life partner by talking to strangers. I've also gained some perspective. It's helped me understand the challenges we face, and the opportunities we have.

Since the start of my first campaign until the end of my latest one, I've knocked on more than 50,000 doors. Maybe some of you have seen me on your doorstep. When you talk to that many strangers you learn a lot. Those strangers' stories and many others have inspired the bills I've sponsored and the votes I've taken in Congress. And in many cases, I'm proud that the strangers I've met on their doorsteps have become friends.

Some lessons you leave behind in childhood. A perfect example is the age old adage "don't talk to strangers." It's the strangers who we have met along the way—those personal relationships we have invested in and those people we've learned from—that bring meaning to our lives.

Number 3: Invest in a zoo membership

As a father, I feel compelled to tell you. … It totally makes sense financially to get a membership to the zoo rather than paying for individual tickets each time you go. Seriously. Particularly for you parents in the audience (or even if you aren't a parent, who doesn't like the zoo?) … if you remember nothing else I say, remember to become a zoo member.

Number 2: Invest in the lives of children

Every night, as I put my daughter to bed I whisper three things in her ear. First, I whisper, "Please sleep through the night." Then I whisper, "Daddy loves you." And finally, I whisper the prayer that I think most parents pray for their kids: "Let us do right by you."

If we want a rosy future for our community, for our country, and for our world, we have got to invest in these little ones. If you're a parent, God bless ya … do all you can for your children. But even if you're not, if you can find some time to invest in kids, it will make a difference.

And here's a key point: You don't have to be a teacher to be a teacher. One of the best examples I can give of this was a Port Angeles legend named Jim Lunt who wasn't a teacher but who taught me a ton. Jim, who recently passed away, was the dad of one of my buddies in school. I started playing pee-wee soccer at age 4, I think. The team I played for was called the Maroon Monsters. Jim did something before each game that I will always remember—in part because it's something that you'd never see someone do these days.

At the start of each game, as we lined up to get the game started, Jim would yell from the sidelines, "Who are we?!?!?"

And we'd all yell, "THE MONSTERS!"

And then, because we had a kid on the team who had a tendency to try to score on our own goal a few too many times, Jim would yell, "Which way are we going?!?!?"

And we'd yell, "THAT WAY!"

And then — and here's the somewhat sketchy part — then he would pull a cigar out of his pocket and lift it proudly in the air. He'd yell, "What is this?!?!?!"

And we'd yell, "THE VICTORY CIGAR!"

And then he'd yell, "And what am I gonna do with it!?!?!"

And we'd yell, "YOU'RE GONNA SMOKE IT!!!!!!"

At the end of each game, win or lose, he'd light

up that cigar because, he told us, we were all winners … and because I believe he had a serious tobacco addiction. Jim wasn't a teacher—but I learned a lot from him. And I wasn't the only one. In the wake of his death, so many people had their own unique Jim story.

I learned how much of a difference it can make to have a caring adult who is willing to give so much of their time and energy.

Number 1: Invest in your community and each other

Finally, we come to my last bit of advice for the evening. I'm glad to see everyone is still glued to their seats. Money is important. It helps pay the rent. It helps with food. It fills the gas tank. It certainly has value. But remember it's not the only thing out there. It's not "All About the Benjamins."

Mother Teresa once said, "Let us not be satisfied with just giving money. Money is not enough; money can be got; but they need your hearts to love them. So, spread your love everywhere you go."

Making more money isn't enough to make us happy—it may be an ingredient, but it's not enough. We all need a sense of purpose—we need to do something rather than to be something.

The all-time best example of this? Paul Revere. If you got a copy of Paul Revere's resumé, his official occupation would be listed as silversmith. That's how he made the money to pay the rent and buy the mutton (or whatever they ate back then). But most people don't know him for what he was, they know him for what he did—and what he did had nothing to do with his job … and he volunteered to do it.

Congratulations on being a select member of the 20 Under 40 club. But remember, this is only one part of you. Remember that your occupation doesn't define you. It's what else you do and who else you are. I'd encourage you to continue to do something rather than to simply be something.

You are already an inspiration to the Kitsap community. Continue that growth. Expand your business and provide more jobs to local workers. Get out there and coach a team of misfit kids that could use a guiding hand. Say hello to the server at your coffee shop, ask how their day is going.

Strengthen your neighborhoods and communities. I know you are already doing great things. And I'm sure more will come. Heck, ten years from now I expect many of you will be ready to stand in my shoes … ready to dispense your own pieces of investment advice.

Thank you, and congratulations.

11

Dr. Gloria Burgess

The Value of Teamwork

Gloria Burgess, Ph.D., was born in Mississippi and grew up there and in Detroit and Ann Arbor, Michigan, the middle child in a family of five girls. In the Burgess family, mom and dad set the expectation that each daughter was headed for college, and Gloria understood that goal. After graduating from the University of Michigan, Gloria went on to earn a master's degree and a doctorate at the University of Southern California. Her initial plan was to pursue a career as a university professor, teaching and conducting research. Instead, she decided to pursue a career in business—in particular, the high-tech business of computers and financial systems.

After two years in technical communications at

Honeywell's computing division, she left for her dream job with the technology division of Citibank. She was soon promoted into management and wound up running the technical publications group.

Gloria had been at Citibank for about two years when she was selected to join the Brazil Tiger Team. At that time in the early 1980s, Citibank was interested in expanding into the international banking markets, and one target of opportunity was Brazil. This was breaking new ground—US banks at that time were just beginning to branch out into multistate networks, and no one in the industry had experience in offshore markets. Gloria was one of the most junior of eight team members selected for the task of studying the project and coming up with recommendations. The CEO of Citibank's Technology Division gave the team marching orders and the date for delivering the final report. They were left to figure out how to proceed and how to deliver a successful report by the deadline, ten weeks away.

Each of the eight team members had different primary skills, including a representative from human resources, a product development engineer, and a systems specialist. Gloria's specialty was technical writing. However, she and her colleagues also had experience in other diverse fields. Gloria had valuable knowledge about human factors, which was useful in creating the final product.

Gloria worked long into the night on several occasions, and even slept under her desk a couple of times. As you have probably guessed, the team completed their project successfully and on time.

I asked Gloria about the lessons she learned from her experience working with a team. Here is her advice (the same applies to any project team):

- A clear purpose and a common goal was defined by management.
- Each of the eight team members understood the assignment.
- They also understood that the stakes were high—the reputation of the Technology Division was on the line.
- It was essential that each member of the team have an equal voice around the table.
- It was a badge of honor to be selected for the team. They didn't want to screw up.
- Each member of the team wanted to learn from the experience.
- It was important to each member that they produce a quality product.
- Each team member needed to be able to trust themselves, and trust the process.

If you are a student, or just getting started in your

career, you might be asking why spend all this time now on discussing Tiger Teams, if you need to be an A player with 10 or 12 years of experience under your belt to qualify for consideration to be selected? The answer is that now is the time to find opportunities to get to know key players, and learn the problem solving process by keeping your eyes open and offering to work on projects or committees.

Gloria explained that she and the other seven members did lots of menial tasks while on the team, but they also had enough clout to call on resources from their home departments and other groups of the division. Even if you had been on the job for only a week, you would be welcomed if you offered to help Gloria edit copy, make copies, or research specific topics, and in the process you would learn and make connections with star players. Once you show willingness to help, it usually doesn't take long for someone to recognize your initiative and find a task or two to hand off to you. Once you complete one task successfully, you are usually handed another. Pretty soon you are a member of the team—perhaps not a member of the starting team, but you will be putting on the same uniform in the same locker room, and be in a position to learn a lot from your teammates.

If you don't find an opportunity to volunteer to help a Tiger Team, look for other ad hoc project committees formed from time to time within your organization. Volunteer to help with the annual United Way drive, or the holiday party committee, or a canned food drive. Get used to working with a team on a common goal, get good at it, and let your management know you appreciate the experience.

12

General George Babbitt

Retired, United States Air Force

An Easy Recipe...

George Babbitt studied mechanical engineering at the University of Washington in the early 1960s. His plan was to spend four years in the U.S. Air Force after graduation, then return to UW for a master's degree prior to joining the family construction business. Toward the end of his four-year service tour, he became concerned about unfavorable conditions in the construction industry, and thought more and more about a career in the Air Force.

George was offered a deal he decided to take—an assignment to the Air Force Institute of Technology at Wright Patterson Air Force Base where he could earn a master's degree while continuing to serve as an officer, with full pay and benefits. In exchange, George agreed to sign up for another four years. He went on to a very successful 35-year career in the Air Force.

When George retired in 2000, the Air Force counted approximately 380,000 members in uniform. At the top of the ladder were about 200 one- and two-star generals, around 20 three-star generals, and at the very top, 11 four-star generals. George was one of the 11 four-stars.

George and his wife, Louise, liked the life of an Air Force family, even though they had 23 addresses in 35 years. George, Louise, and their two children appreciated the sense of adventure and the stimulation of living in different places in the United States and Europe.

This is a very significant point. Not only is success in a large organization related to how well you like your job—whether it is the Air Force or Starbucks or Boeing—it is also related to whether your career suits your spouse and family well.

George stressed the importance of finding a good fit:

> Pick a career path that you find interesting and challenging. If you begin each day bored and uninterested in what lies ahead, if your mind is always on something else, then find a new career.

He also explained that some of his fellow officers resigned at the middle levels of their careers because their families did not like the Air Force career, with frequent relocations and sometimes being left behind.

Finding a career that is interesting and challenging, and one that is a good fit for your family, are only some of the factors in the success formula. Let's take a look at what George said about the attributes, talents, beliefs and skills that helped him succeed in his career.

Preparation. George did not attend the Air Force Academy, nor was he a pilot. He didn't grow up in a family where the father was a career officer in the armed services. George was an engineer by training, and he credits what he learned in engineering school as a valuable contributor to his career success. He often used the engineering method of analyzing a problem and designing a solution while serving as an Air Force officer.

It is clear that George's undergraduate engineering studies, coupled with his Master of Science degree in logistics management at the Air Force Institute of Technology, helped him prepare for senior management positions with extremely broad responsibilities.

George described several significant positions he held as an Air Force general:

> In 1997 I was promoted to 4-star General and placed in command of the Air Force Materiel Command (AFMC) headquartered in Dayton, Ohio. I reported to the Chief of Staff of the Air Force. AFMC was responsible for conducting research and development, test and evaluation, acquisition, and logistics support for the Air Force.

> Engineering, program management, supply chain management, and equipment maintenance were the key disciplines of the command. Budget reductions and downsizing were a key activity in the 1990s. In 1997, AFMC employed about 105,000 people, of which about 70% were civil servants. When I retired in 2000, AFMC employed about 85,000. Mission support was always our highest priority, but cost management was an increasingly important goal.
>
> I also had two jobs as a 3-star which I thought were important. I served as the Deputy Chief of Staff for Logistics at Headquarters Air Force and as Director of the Defense Logistics Agency (DLA). DLA was an activity of Department of Defense and was responsible for acquisition and distribution of commercially available products for all the military services.

This raises a couple of points important to understand: 1) Leading an organization of 100,000 plus employees is a very large job; 2) the mission at AFMC was complex and technical, requiring extremely capable leaders with excellent educational preparation, plus 30 plus years of experience and on-the-job training to succeed, especially at a time when budgets and headcount were being reduced.

The most talented person in the world would not succeed in a role like this even if they were also the luckiest person around, without the right kind of preparation.

Earn success on the job. This advice can be practiced every day of your career, from your first week at work, and also 35 years later. It isn't complicated, and it may not always be easy, but it will help you succeed, especially in a large organization.

George shared some thoughts on this:

» Stay focused on making the organization you are part of successful. It will be noticed.

» Learn everything you can about the organization you are part of. The old adage that I'm a manager (or leader) and I can manage (or lead) anything is not true.

» Seek out jobs that interest you and that you can do well.

» Remember that being selected for a job is an opportunity not a reward. You need to succeed or you may not get the next job.

» Find an operational problem you think you can fix (most organizations have quite a few) and volunteer to lead a task force to come up with a solution. This will earn you a reputation as a doer—a planner and problem solver.

» So long as you continue to do well with your primary job, your management and the organization will look for more opportunities for you to solve more problems and do more.

Daily practices. George also shared techniques to maintain interest and improve job performance.

» Every career has a daily routine. Don't let the routine things become an issue by leaving them undone.

» Pay attention to your team members. Help them; teach them.

» Constantly assess what are the biggest challenges facing your boss and his boss. Spend part of each day working your boss's problems.

High-performing teams. There are operations in government, the armed services, and in business that are best accomplished by high-performing teams composed of individuals who train together and commit to achieve challenging team goals. You might think of Navy SEAL teams, surgical teams in an operating room, or EMTs who respond when someone dials 911 for help with a suspected heart attack. High-performing teams are often operating in an environment which is challenging, unpredictable, sometimes dangerous, and where the job must be completed quickly. Constant measurement and continuous improvement are generally part of the high-performing team environment. Working in such an environment can be an extremely rewarding career experience.

I asked George to describe a high-performing team he worked with in the Air Force:

> The teams were called Integrated Combat Turn (ICT) teams. Their goal was to recover an air defense fighter aircraft in a combat situation, park it inside a hardened aircraft shelter, inspect it for damage or malfunction, refuel it, and re-arm it (eight new missiles) safely—and within 15 minutes.
>
> Team procedures and processes were reviewed and updated regularly by a lead team (Standardization & Evaluation) and then approved by local commanders. New members went through initial individual training and then through team training when they were assigned to a team. All teams trained weekly, actually loading, refueling an aircraft. Once a quarter the wing conducted a simulated combat exercise lasting at least three days.
>
> This was a dangerous environment: F-15 aircraft in tight quarters, highly volatile fuel, live weapons, and speed. It was similar to a pit stop in auto racing. In my experience the teams always stayed focused on safety. They met and constantly exceeded the standards for speed.

Leadership. Defining the traits and qualities that add up to effective leadership can be very tricky. If a personality could be analyzed or a test could be devised to identify successful future leaders, the armed services and Fortune 500 would be doing this routinely. The fact is, the best indicator of successful leadership may be simply looking at would-be leaders to see if anyone is following them. If there were a way to select successful future leaders, the Air Force would be using it, and the pattern of new officers struggling with their first leadership roles would not be repeated year after year.

In the Air Force, the first test a new, 22-year old second lieutenant might face would be to lead a group of 50 or so enlisted men and non-commissioned officers. According to George, in an aircraft maintenance wing environment the enlisted men and NCOs were highly skilled with years of experience under their belts. The new second lieutenants were not.

In practice, what happened year after year was the performance of the new officers fell into three categories.

The successful new officers were those who established good working relationships with the NCOs, learned from them, and in some cases encouraged the NCOs to mentor them. They were able to identify issues or problems faced by their group that they could tackle and make a difference. Officers in this category received positive promotion recommendations.

The second group of prospective leaders were clueless and could not figure out their roles. They were not identified as future leaders.

The third group wanted to exercise all of the prerogatives of leadership without understanding how to fashion a positive role for themselves. They chose the wrong priorities, such as insisting that all airmen and NCOs follow dress regulations and other rules to the letter, without an understanding of the operational obligations of the group. Officers in this category were, as you would expect, not recommended for leadership roles.

George had quite a bit to discuss about leadership. His thoughts:

> Over the years I have come to believe that there are few, if any, physical, mental, or personality traits that reliably describe a leader. In the end, a leader is someone the group follows.
>
> I believe leadership is defined within the context of an organization. A leader in one situation may not be effective in another. To be a leader you need to love the organization you are part of and its mission. You need to understand the goals of that organization and be able to translate them into meaningful actions for the group you are responsible for. Your team members need to follow and your combined actions must result in a measure of success. You will be seen then as a leader and, more than likely, offered another opportunity to lead.
>
> A leader can't be a screamer. You need to be able to control your temper. In most cases you should focus on gathering all the facts by communicating

> with all involved parties. But then you have to make a decision, and move on.
>
> I would rule out all abusive behavior, physical or mental. There will always be some abusive individuals who succeed, but I believe that is often because their other skills overwhelm the negative aspects of their abusiveness. Treat people fairly; help and teach them; and where necessary, discipline them.
>
> Team building is essential, but make sure your team is inclusive and doesn't become a clique. Build consensus. As the boss, there will be the temptation to just give orders. In an emergency, this may be both appropriate and essential. But in many other situations, giving orders limits new ideas and eliminates the opportunity to teach. When you give orders, the group will obey, but don't mistake this for leadership.

It is important to say about the business of leadership that not everyone is going to be happy or successful in a leadership position. A few years ago, I was involved in a dynamic nationwide insurance agency and I got to know and admire our top salesman, who regularly turned in three to five times the business of average successful agents. This person was a sales superman, earning a super income plus the respect of hundreds of agents across the country who would try to copy his style and techniques. Very few knew or remembered that only a few years earlier this all-star had spent a miserable and unsuccessful year in the role of a sales manager, which simply was not a good fit.

We have a lot to say in this book about leadership because organizations always need more effective leaders, and successful leaders are rewarded by these organizations. However, your choice may be research scientist, playing first violin in the symphony, or being a successful insurance agent. If the right fit for you is a career as an individual contributor, then go for it and don't be tempted to switch to a leadership role.

Boil down George's advice to the basics, and it looks like a simple recipe for success:

» Select a career that you find interesting and challenging.

» Spend time learning the organization; its purpose, goals, challenges and history.

» Do well in the job you have.

» Spend time each day working on solutions to your boss's problems.

The last question I submitted to George was this: *Not everyone is as successful as you have been. What do you think you had going for you that allowed you to be more successful than some of your peers?*

George's response:

Luck played an important part. In a large institution

> like the US Air Force, success is defined as continually moving up through the ranks. Moving up through the ranks requires that you be successful in your current job. But not all jobs are equal. Some are seen by the institution as more important than others. So, along the way you need to be selected for those difficult jobs.
>
> I can honestly say that each time I was selected for one of those 'important' jobs I was surprised. Every time, I knew others that I considered more qualified than myself."

General Babbitt had one more very thoughtful comment about his philosophy of leadership:

> I never saw my rank or position as entitling. I saw rank and position as a charge and responsibility to serve. I believe organizations inside and outside of government would be better led if more individuals adopted this approach.

13

Dave Stevens

Start out Poor…

Dave Stevens and his wife, Catherine, moved to the Pacific Northwest to be near their children and grandchildren, and the best boating in the world. Dave retired at the age of 58 from a major Canadian-based international mining company, where he was senior vice president of international exploration, supervising a team of 120 professionals, with a $75 million annual budget.

Dave and Catherine have been a team for more than 50 years, and can enjoy their good health, families, travel, boating and many other interests because they worked together to achieve success. But it wasn't a slam dunk for them.

Dave grew up poor in Stockton, a small city in central

California. His father had multiple sclerosis and was very ill for years prior to his death in 1961, shortly after Dave graduated from high school. His mother was the breadwinner, and was determined that her only child would attend college and become successful.

Dave says that growing up poor was a powerful motivator because the only way to go was up! His description of his college career is interesting:

> I spent a semester in a junior college after high school, joined the National Guard (because a bunch of high school buddies did), spent six months on active duty, had a real look at the world and came to the personal realization—to my mother's great relief—that a college education was required for any personal or financial success. I reentered junior college and took all sorts of classes, including Russian, engineering, chemistry and geology.
>
> Geology fascinated me and after working in a placer gold mining "scheme" (the guy who hired me mined investors while I sucked meager amounts of gold from a river bed in the Sierras), I decided to make it my profession.
>
> I talked my way into the University of Nevada in Reno in 1963, nearly flunked out after the first semester, got married and stayed on the dean's list until graduation in 1966, with a bachelor's in geological engineering.

Talking with Dave about his undergraduate experience, I asked what caused the dramatic turnaround, from nearly flunking out of the University of Nevada to qualifying for the dean's list and earning his degree. He says it was all due to marrying Catherine at age 21. He suddenly felt responsible for becoming successful. His wife, a teacher earning $750 per month, was supporting him and he knew it was time for him to concentrate on his studies and prepare for a professional career. So no more going out nights with the boys. It was time to focus on accomplishing things, like a college degree and finding a good job.

His advice on picking the right partner:

> Pick a good life-partner and never underestimate the value of mentors! My wife's unflagging support got me through college, and her willingness to drag our young family all over the world as I took on new jobs was what, more than anything, led to our success.

Dave looks like he enjoys life and he has a well-developed sense of humor. He also looks like the head coach, the guy in charge, the man with the whistle. He is friendly, decisive, verbal and quick, and he creates the impression of a person who doesn't take himself too seriously, but at the same time possesses almost limitless self-confidence.

Dave finds It easy to step up to leadership opportunities, and he gave a lot of thought to how to develop an effective leadership style:

I have always been somewhat extroverted and drawn to leadership roles. With only nine years of experience, I was selected by my supervisor/mentor to manage a joint venture in Ireland. This was my first management responsibility, there was no local staff, and I was totally unprepared. I tried to imagine how I would react to an Irishman showing up and offering me a job in Nevada. I always made it a mental point to first be the person I was talking to, before talking to them. As it turned out, the only cultural standoff was over what time work started—8:00 a.m. or 10:00 a.m. Sharing a "jar" of Guinness at the local pub at my expense at the end of the day prevailed, and the workday began at 8:00.

Over the ensuing years my management responsibility increased, but early on it occurred to me that management was more about mentoring and determining how to get the most out of people, than providing technical guidance. To do that, you needed to know people fairly well. Mutual respect is essential.

With each new management job, I read all of the current books on successful management, the importance of teams, and handling crisis situations. In all honesty, they weren't all that useful, other than hearing about others' problems and how to avoid them.

I would emphasize the importance of maintaining a reasonable number of direct

> reports—less than 10—so that you really get to know them, understand their strengths and needs, and plan training in areas that need improvement. In a quiet one on one moment, free of distractions, asking "tell me what you do" was a great barrier breaker in getting to know someone and far more useful than a formalized job description.
>
> The identification of problem areas, whether it is an individual or a reporting structure, and taking quick action to remedy the problem is a valuable attribute. This was exceptionally important during the times in my career when I found myself in a new organization working with new people.

Dave's career included several international assignments, in addition to the mine in Ireland. In his last position as senior vice president of international exploration, Dave was managing a multi-national team working in nine different countries around the world. Here's how he handled it:

> My direct reports were from various countries and backgrounds. I thought of my principle responsibility as an "enabler"—to create an environment of maximum productivity and creativity for them and their reports. This involved getting to know each person and his family on a fairly personal basis.
>
> The success of this effort, which included the discovery of three major mines, also led to the company being acquired by a larger one and me

> losing my job. Rather than spending another five to seven years flying around the world and chasing potential mines, we decided to retire, moved to the Pacific Northwest and bought a boat.

Dave came to understand that successful mining operations required more than science, exploration, analysis, and poking holes in the ground. This was not a business where wildcatters wandered across the hills and mountains hoping to luck out and find a mother lode. Developing a new mining site is incredibly expensive—hundreds of millions of dollars—and the money must often be raised from investment banks and directors who don't trust to luck. They want feasibility studies and the confirming data that convince them the new mine will be a good long-term investment—pay back the money they contributed, plus a profit.

Investors fund the companies and projects that have the most believable, the most professional, best documented plans. Results are always clear and objective and since we are talking here about hundreds of millions of dollars, everyone keeps score. The business of finding ore deposits, evaluating new mining opportunities on the basis of long term return on investment, is known as economic geology.

Dave explained how he became interested in this early in his career:

> My career started as a geologist working in the hills of central Nevada. At that point, I realized that there was a lot more to my chosen profession than what is

learned in the classroom. I was eager to get as much experience as quickly as possible. I was offered a job working for a USAID contractor in India that we declined, upon learning that Catherine was pregnant with our first of three children.

By age 25, I had built a mobile analytical laboratory, as getting rapid sample results was the biggest bottleneck in mineral exploration. I did not, however, share my supervisor's view that I should become an analytical technician, so I began searching for another job and more money.

Thanks largely to a benevolent mentor, I went to work for an extremely well-funded fledgling mineral exploration company, a division of EXXON, that led to progressively more responsibility and a management position by age 30.

At about this time, I started to develop a strong interest in the financial aspects of mining, and a realization that these considerations played an important role in determining and guiding an exploration program. Developing a broader view of the mining industry was instrumental to my professional development.

Dave credits much of his early career success to the mentoring he received from professors, supervisors and his colleagues:

A professor, who I worked for part time (he was

> an industry consultant on the side), suggested a company that was just opening a copper mine in central Nevada near the delightful community of Battle Mountain, about half way between Reno and Salt Lake City.
>
> From a standard of living point, it was only uphill from there. My job was to supervise drilling, analyze the results, and make estimates of the mining reserves for the engineering department.
>
> The head of that company was recruited by what was later renamed EXXON, and he recruited me three years later. Over a 35-year career, five different companies employed me and we moved 14 times, each to a new and more interesting/challenging job in the minerals exploration industry.

Reading this you probably get a sense of a dynamic and very successful career, with many moves, jobs, locations and challenges. Dave was a very successful geologist, manager and leader, and I am highly confident that he enjoys every one of his birthdays, as well as other special moments with his family and friends. He's worked hard, become very successful, enjoys a good life and he's earned it all.

I asked Dave for some general advice for people starting out on their career journey and this is what he had to say:

- Work with people you like and respect. Socializing is an important management tool. Become an enabler to others.

- Attack the task at hand with the best of your abilities; focus on it and not what it might lead to.

- Do not put off problems, either technical or people; they will not heal themselves and will likely get worse if untreated.

- Seek opportunities to diversify your professional experiences. Make sure you sample enough career experiences to narrow the field.

- Do what you truly find interesting, both intellectually and socially. It may take a while, but it is the most important commitment you will make — other than marriage — and it lasts a lifetime, so give yourself every opportunity to get it right. You do not want to be 30-something, married, with kids, well-mortgaged, and wake up in the middle of the night realizing that your job really sucks.

- Pick a profession that you will always have an interest in, and passion for.

14

Jim Burns

A Family Business

When asked to describe the town where he lives, Jim Burns says it this way: "Syracuse is a comfortable, small to mid-sized city. The people are friendly, and there are a lot of things to do. It is also a great place to raise a family." Jim has lived there nearly 50 years and he has family in Syracuse—as well as the family business, started by his father in 1974—so has no plans to leave. He has served as chief executive officer of the investment counseling firm, J.W. Burns & Company, for the past 16 years.

Jim grew up in a middle-class neighborhood, the youngest of three kids. He enjoyed sports, and the lacrosse and basketball teams he played on in high school earned all-county honors. During his freshman and sophomore years,

Jim was elected class president, but he didn't run for the office in his junior year. Jim wasn't sure he wanted to run for class president in his senior year, either, and was doubtful that he could win if he did. His dad encouraged him to give it a try. He did, and was elected. His father's ability to help Jim build the confidence needed to become successful was evident.

Jim's dad also coached him to become an effective public speaker. The most important advice from his father on public speaking:

> First, take the time for proper preparation.
> Second, brevity is important and can be an advantage.
> Third, don't try to impress: instead, connect!

Following high school, Jim went on to earn a Bachelor of Arts degree in communications and journalism from St. John Fisher College, where he also played basketball. After graduation, he moved to Boston and a job with an ad agency. He continued to develop communications skills by joining Toastmasters. After several years on his own, he decided to return to J.W. Burns & Company in Syracuse to work with his father and learn the business.

The first lesson was a shocker—the stock market crashed that year. The Dow Jones Industrial Average peaked in August 1987 at 2,722, up a rousing 44% over the close on the last trading day of 1986. However, international markets were unstable and crazy things were happening around the world. Iran fired missiles at two unarmed American-flagged oil tankers in the Middle East. The United States responded by shelling an Iranian oil platform. In mid- October, markets around the world began selling off, and on Monday, October 19, 1987, markets in the United States registered their largest decline ever, dropping 508 points to 1,738—down 22% from the August peak. This has been memorialized by referring to the date and the event as Black Monday.

You can imagine that Jim must have been discouraged when his first year in the business included the worst decline US investors had ever experienced. But he got up, dusted himself off, and went back to work.

Again, Jim's dad gave him very clear advice:

- Read and absorb information about business, markets, politics, and foreign policy.
- Get to really know and understand your business.
- To build confidence, Just do it!
- Focus on progress, not perfection.

Jim developed a philosophy while he was learning the business: "I will study. I will learn. I will prepare. And someday I may have a chance to apply this."

His dad was delighted that Jim wanted to join him in the investment business, but he also made it clear that Jim needed to prove himself. In addition to studying, learning, and absorbing the details of the business, Jim was expected to bring in new business by attracting new clients, and he was expected to recommend good stock picks.

Jim believed he could also help by applying marketing and communications skills he learned in college, and during his time at the ad agency. He seized the opportunity to apply his marketing talents to the business, while learning the investment and client service side from his father. They worked together to develop a plan of attack.

In 1989, there were no Chartered Financial Analysts in Syracuse. As described in Helen Stewart's story in Chapter 6, earning a CFA charter is no easy task. More than 50% who sit for the series of exams fail the first time. Given the credibility in the investment world as a CFA charterholder, Jim's dad thought the designation would give Jim a significant competitive advantage to become one of the first CFAs in town. Like Helen Stewart, and Kent Weymouth in a following chapter, Jim spent four years studying, learning and preparing to successfully pass the three exams to earn his Chartered Financial Analyst designation.

While learning to master public speaking, Jim developed a deep, low voice which sounded confident and more mature than someone just a few years out of college. He found he was able to connect with prospects over the phone, and scheduled face-to-face appointments. When he showed up on their doorsteps, they often remarked that they expected someone older.

Jim connected well with people, and used his strong

communication skills to sell the "sizzle" of the J.W. Burns story, the portfolio of great companies they invested in, and the performance of that portfolio over the years. He loved building the business by bringing in new clients, and he was motivated—he wanted to buy a house of his own and needed to earn more money to do it. More clients meant more earnings. He was on it, and he liked it.

Another area of focus was stock picking—selecting great companies to invest in, companies that would provide a superior return for J.W. Burns investors through dividend payments and the appreciation of their stock price. One of Jim's first picks was Philip Morris. He was reading The Wall Street Journal one day and found a positive article about the company and their 16 percent year-on-year growth. He was impressed, and worked up a presentation on Phillip Morris and pitched it to his father. The elder Burns approved.

Next, Jim's reading and research turned up Stryker Laboratories in Kalamazoo, Michigan, manufacturers of medical devices and equipment. Jim's dad liked the analysis Jim prepared and encouraged him to visit Stryker to get a feel for the operation. He did, and they soon began buying Stryker stock for client portfolios.

In addition to being a student of the business, bringing in new clients, and picking great stocks, Jim also began to build the J.W. Burns brand by using his marketing and communications skills. He remembers with great satisfaction pitching stories about J.W. Burns to the Syracuse newspaper and to financial magazines. His first big success was with Barron's, where he was able to attract the attention of

Kate Welling, who wrote about investment gurus. The story was simple: a father-son team of investment counselors in Syracuse was growing their business and their clients' wealth by picking great companies to invest in.

In addition to getting positive stories printed in magazines and newspapers, Jim started a quarterly client newsletter. Over the years, he has become very successful in obtaining media coverage in respected publications, such as The Wall Street Journal, Barron's, Central New York Business Journal, and Forbes Online. Jim is also author of a monthly column, "Investors Edge", published in the Syracuse Post Standard. For several years, he co-hosted Financial Fitness, a television show broadcast on WCNY, a New York PBS station. He has applied his marketing and communications skills very effectively to the family business.

Jim also learned some helpful lessons from colleagues, which he relies upon today.

> When I was a stock broker early on in my career, it was hard to build a business and I was struggling. One day, a friend suggested I write down a list of at least 35 things in my life to be grateful for, and to read this list every morning and every night.
>
> I did this, and to this day I believe in the power of gratitude to create positive energy, focus, and success. I still aggressively practice gratitude on a daily basis. The daily practice of gratitude is a keystone in the success I have enjoyed, and I highly recommend it.

Jim's father passed away in 1999. Jim remembers him as a gentleman and a great mentor. He will always remember the following advice from his dad:

> *Successful people are always trying to learn and to grow.*

Asked what recommendations he had for people seeking successful careers, Jim had a lot to contribute:

> I would continue to read, study and learn as much as you can in the field in which you work. Be better informed than your competitors and, in fact, than everyone. Learn more to earn more.

Follows is my Q & A with Jim:

What are your tips on leadership?

> I truly believe that reading top-notch, self-improvement or motivational literature is vital to learning, growing and staying motivated, and learning how to lead.
>
> Model successful people. In my case, I continue to try to model my father, who was a great human being and a very successful investor.

What makes a mentor effective?

> A helpful mentor would be anyone whom you respect, trust and is ahead of you in the game of life.

What lessons did you learn early in your career that helped you succeed?

Watching my father taught me the value of being unemotional and dispassionate when investing. I observed how he kept his cool during many bear markets and scary times, and this, I believe, is a skill and practice that I have learned.

As an investment manager, one of the key skills is to think outside the box, or expect the unexpected.

What do you think most contributed to your success in your business?

A positive attitude every day; hard work; and making the effort to get along with others and develop great working relationships have been indispensable. Good working relationships and a strong reputation are vital, as is the ability to execute.

As Warren Buffet said, "One's objective should be get it right, get it done, get it quick, get it out, and get it over."

I want to add some perspective to Jim's story. He leads a small team at J.W. Burns & Company, fewer than a dozen. They manage investments for more than 450 clients, any of which can decide on any day to close their accounts and take their business elsewhere. Total funds under management equal about half a billion dollars.

Every quarter, the firm sends a report to each client with

a scorecard: How well did my investments do in the past 90 days? So far this year? Compared to last year? Compared to the Dow Jones Industrial Average? Compared to Standard and Poor's?

Jim may have inherited the business his father built, but that fact doesn't help him with the quarterly report cards and the comparisons with the various market indexes. He has been successful on his own for 16 years, through all the highs and lows of the stock market. I wanted his story in this book because his career is a lot like being a pro golfer—his name is on the leader board, and his score is posted along with all of his rivals. His clients know that he won't be at the top every day, but they are counting on him to perform well over a long period of time so that their investments, their hard-earned cash, can grow to pay for important things like college educations for kids and grandkids, retirement, and all the other expenses of life.

Very few careers have the same kind of public performance measurement as running an investment business. Even professional athletes can have successful careers without performing at Hall of Fame levels. But investing clients' money is different. Every client wants and needs superior performance. Every client is looking for a super-star team to build their wealth.

It doesn't surprise me that Jim's final words of advice include the 'get it right, get it done, get it out quote' from Warren Buffet.

The investment business doesn't fit everyone. Many people will decide that the risks are too great or too frequent, or that the continuous measurement and the public reporting of performance on a scoreboard next to your competitors is not appealing. The purpose of including Jim's story is to focus on the important factors he parlayed into success in his business:

» Preparation

» Continual learning

» Find effective mentors

» Hard work

» Learn how to work well with others

By now, these factors should sound familiar.

15

Barbara Malich

"We're going to motor out of the harbor and turn left..."

Barbara Malich, CEO of Peninsula Community Health Services (PCHS) in Bremerton, Washington, for the past 22 years, plans to retire within the next year. When I asked what she and her husband Ken, also retired, were planning to do after her retirement party, she said they plan to get on their boat, putt out of the harbor, and head north—up Puget Sound to the San Juan and Gulf Islands, and the lovely ports and cruising areas that stretch all the way to Alaska.

People who know Barb, and know the story of her career, are not surprised that she plans to take off without a detailed plan or agenda. For nearly forty-five years she has been zig-zagging across the world, landing and succeeding in jobs that are different—such as, lobbyist; executive secretary of the National Tire Dealers and Retreaders Association; a teacher in Lahore, Pakistan, and Kuala Lumpur, Malaysia; and, back in the U.S., a substitute teacher—to mention just a few of the positions she held before she became CEO of the health center.

As you will learn in this chapter, some of her moves were motivated by career opportunities, some by romance, and some by a spirit of adventure. You might say that in her career she played a good game of bridge, making the best of the cards she was dealt, and won the top spot at PCHS, where she was able to satisfy her passion for providing health care services to low-income and uninsured citizens of the community.

Peninsula Community Health Services, a non-profit organization, provides primary medical care, dental care, behavioral health counseling, pharmacy services, referrals to specialty providers, and health education and promotion activities in five health centers located in and around Bremerton and Poulsbo, Washington. Health care services are provided without regard for a patient's ability to pay. Although these towns are less than 20 miles across Puget Sound from Seattle, as the seagull flies, they are perched on the eastern rims of the Kitsap and Olympic peninsulas. If you want to visit the Seattle metro area, you face a one-hour ferry ride or a two-hour plus drive to get there.

Life in Kitsap County is very different from life in Seattle Metro. The local economy is still struggling to rebound from the slump in the timber and plywood businesses and the miseries of 2007-2008. Employment opportunities lag those found in the metro area. Hospitals and medical centers are scarce, and so is public transportation. The region attracts retirees, but they don't generate many middle-class or high-income jobs.

PCHS is a federally-qualified facility, so there is abundant regulation and paperwork. There is also no shortage of low-income, no-income and uninsured citizens who need medical help—last year PCHS recorded 75,000 patient visits. The total staff is approximately 150 persons.

The CEO job is a big job. Let's take a look at Barbara's career prior to joining PCHS to examine the path she followed to the CEO spot at age 43.

Barbara was born in Missouri and raised in Nebraska until age 9, when her family moved to Wyoming. She earned a Bachelor of Arts in English and education at University of Wyoming at age 21.

Here's how Barb describes her college years:

> I was bribed by my parents with a trip to Europe after high school graduation if I would stay in Laramie and attend the University of Wyoming for at least two years—in-state tuition was cheap then and I had scholarships, as well. I took the bait!
>
> I attended the University of Wyoming, majored in American Studies, and then shifted to English, with a teaching certificate. I had a great time in college. I was active in a sorority (compensation for staying in-state); nurtured many different interests (played

> clarinet in the university band); encountered my first real experiences in leadership—president of the student union, my sorority, and several other wonderful leadership experiences.

From this account of college, we begin to get the picture of a young woman taking advantage of many different opportunities while at college—academic, social, and even political—and gaining some leadership experience, as well. It is likely that not everything Barbara attempted was successful, but she was successful enough that she began to develop a self-confidence that helped propel through some interesting and valuable career adventures in her future, and even helped her to follow her heart fifteen years later to travel with the man she fell in love with across the continent and to a new life in the Pacific Northwest.

Barbara knew while still in high school that her parents expected her to complete college and perhaps also earn a graduate degree, but she was not enthusiastic about the limited career opportunities for educated women at the time—teaching or nursing. Her parents, both teachers with master's degrees, prevailed on her to earn a teaching certificate as a career life-preserver. She did, and she was surprised to find out during her stint at student teaching that she liked it. It was as if she had been dealt a "teaching" card and, as you will read, she played it well.

Armed with her teaching certificate, Barbara headed for Nebraska to begin her working career. She found the overall employment package in Nebraska to be attractive, and for the next two years enjoyed work in the classroom. But it wasn't long before a sense of adventure influenced her to begin researching teaching opportunities abroad. Through networking, she learned that the former superintendent of schools in Laramie was now headmaster of the Lahore American Society School in Pakistan. With his support she landed a two-year teaching assignment in Lahore, followed by two years teaching in an American school in Kuala Lumpur.

Next, Barbara applied to the United States Foreign Service, but it didn't work out, so she returned to the United States, settled in with an aunt in Tucson, and worked as a substitute teacher. She was biding time, planning the next steps in her career path.

Barbara decided on a graduate degree program at American University in Washington, D.C., where she would find a job to pay the bills and pursue her degree during her off hours. Her studies led to a Master of Science in public relations. She found work first with the National Center for Administrative Justice, followed by jobs with the National Tire Dealers and Retreaders Association; National Nurses Association; and American College of Obstetricians and Gynecologists.

All of these organizations had a common goal—representing the interests of their members across the country to lawmakers in Congress and the policymakers in the Executive Branch. In her last position in Washington, Barbara was active in fundraising, seeking federal grant support, establishing relationships with foundations and public corporations, and with specialized medical practice groups. Her advanced degree in public relations helped her land the job, and her experience in the role would turn out to be very helpful to her in landing the CEO job with PCHS a few years later.

Shortly after Barbara started with the American College of Obstetricians and Gynecologists, one of her colleagues, a woman who grew up in Washington State, set her up on a blind date with her brother, Ken. To make this happen, she had to convince Ken to fly 3,000 miles from the Seattle area to Washington, D.C. And it worked. Barbara and Ken clicked, decided to marry, and she found herself headed for the Pacific Northwest to wed Ken and begin the next stage of her career.

When I interviewed Barbara, I asked several questions about how she developed the self-confidence she needed to travel to new places, find new jobs, and make progress in her career while bouncing all over the map. She recalled her mother's life, raising her brother Bob, and then beginning a teaching career so she would have the money needed for his college education.

Barbara was also influenced by several aunts who were successful, independent women with careers that included teaching at the university level. Her leadership experiences in college also helped prepare her for her career, but perhaps most important were the skills she developed as a teacher.

How does she define the job of a teacher? Communication! In her own words: "I don't believe I have ever stopped being an educator … communications and teaching are the keys to my success."

Spend ten minutes in conversation with Barbara and you will see that she has impressive communication skills. She speaks clearly, looks you in the eye, and listens and responds to what you have to say. She also writes well, and she manages to transmit a friendly, positive impression, free of ego or self-importance.

Barbara was stumped after she left the east coast for Washington State. But not for long. Within a few months she was hired as executive director by YWCA of Kitsap County. She described her work for a community program, Alternatives to Living in a Violent Environment (ALIVE):

> The ALIVE program, which provides shelter and support services for victims of domestic violence, is the primary program. During my tenure, we created legal advocacy programs and comprehensive support systems for children caught in the cycle of violence.

Barbara spent three years with the YWCA, then a new opportunity opened up in a field she cared about and understood—community health care.

> Peninsula Community Health Services had just been funded in the fall of 1993 as a federally qualified health center, and I was fortunate to lead PCHS through a period of tremendous growth, which continues today.

To help complete the picture, follows are a few questions and answers, and advice from my interviews and correspondence with Barbara:

What other experiences helped prepare you for a successful career?

Both of my parents were teachers, so during the summers we had the chance to take some longer trips. They required my participation in great conversations; challenged my curiosity about travel, in both domestic and foreign destinations; and taught me how to listen and communicate.

Do you have specific recommendations for people seeking successful careers?

The times are very different now. Many more opportunities and many more challenges face young people today. I think looking at how to succeed and what skills are needed to be successful are important.I don't believe the formal (multiple degrees) college education is as important as it used to be. But I do believe communication skills, active listening, and building a sense of support for those we may perceive as less fortunate is essential.

Making a difference in a person's life is the most rewarding thing anyone can experience—perhaps as a parent, or a teacher, or someone who devotes themselves to social/human services.

How would you suggest that young people develop leadership skills?

Involvement in student government, social clubs, like-minded friends and peers, and cultivating mentors who will serve as guides, if needed, are tools that come to mind.

Will you describe an example of a helpful mentor?

In my current position, my most helpful mentors have been fellow CEOs of community health centers across the state and throughout the region. We are a pretty tight-knit group, and we have learned from each other.

Together, in the early 1990s, Washington State community health centers created a Medicaid insurance company (Community Health Plan of Washington). We learned from skilled staff we hired, we made mistakes, we challenged each other to succeed, and we forged political alliances and personal friendships that continue today.

Understanding this increasingly complex industry has been our opportunity and our challenge. We had to identify our role and forge ahead!

At times that type of action is described as a "leap of faith"—and to a certain extent, I agree. But it was also a deliberate decision to succeed and then to lead each other into that success.

How do you describe your leadership style?

My senior staff would describe my leadership style as "intuitive"—but I prefer to call it observational. Watch, listen, learn, stay connected, and try to anticipate the future as much as possible.

Can you describe your senior team and how it functions?

Members. Nine high-performing individuals who won't accept anything other than success for PCHS: CEO (chief operating officer), COO (chief operating officer), CFO (chief financial officer), CIO (chief informations officer), quality director, medical and dental directors, and human resources director.

Culture. Throughout the organization, we have created a culture where the expectation is that everyone works to the top of their license, or skill set. That has resulted in strong, integrated teams that are engaged in identifying opportunities and facing challenges with optimism and support for each other.

Not everyone is as successful as you have been. What do you think you had going for you that allowed you to be more successful than some of your peers?

I came to this job with some maturity ... and then stuck to it. I bounced around quite a bit when I was younger—and that was good, too—but all those early experiences led me to this position, where I have succeeded beyond my wildest dreams.

15

Phil Caruthers

"It's not at all like winning the lottery..."

Winning the lottery doesn't take much effort. All you need to do is visit a retail store that sells lottery tickets, take out your money, and buy a ticket. After that, all you can do is trust in your luck, because the odds of winning—for example, a share of a Powerball Jackpot—are roughly 175 million to one. You can improve your odds by buying more than one ticket, but there isn't anything else you can do to make it more likely that you will win. Odds are you won't win, so buying lottery tickets is not a good plan for achieving financial success.

Nearly sixty years ago in the town of Harlingen, Texas, in the Rio Grande Valley, Phil Caruthers was almost afraid to open the letter he held in his hand, sent from Rice University in Houston. If the letter from the admissions office said *yes,* he would be on his way to an education at one of the most elite technical universities—and where tuition was free at the time—and he would have a good chance to expand his horizons past the limitations of his childhood. If the message was *no,* he would be headed for a community college that he could afford.

Phil opened the envelope, the answer was *yes*, and for a moment he felt like he had won the Irish Sweepstakes (Powerball had not yet been invented) and his world had changed. But unlike a lottery winner, he worked hard to improve his odds for success.

The oldest of four brothers, Phil was born in south Texas. His family moved to Harlingen, a town of 30,000, when he was in the ninth grade. His mom was a teacher for a time, and his father was a school superintendent until he bought a small shipyard. There was never quite enough money for all the things a young family needed.

By the time Phil enrolled in high school, he wanted a better life and a different future for himself, and he possessed enough self-confidence and determination to try to make that happen. He worked hard in school and earned outstanding grades.

In his senior year, he was salutatorian—number two academically in his class. Only two graduating seniors from his school were accepted by Rice: Phil, and the valedictorian, the number one student. The odds were not 175 million to one, but there were only two winners from that town in Texas, and they had both worked hard and earned their success.

Phil would probably tell you that leadership ability is not in his DNA, but as you will learn from his story, he was a very successful leader and manager during his career. His preparation for being a successful leader began as early as high school, where he was president of the school band. He was also the leader, founder, and chief organizer of a dance band, where he played saxophone. In college, Phil was quarterback on an intramural football team. All of these activities, supplemented by his innate talents, and the preparation and investments he made in graduate school and through on-the-job training, gave him the confidence and experience to function as a successful leader.

One lesson to be learned from his experiences is that seeking out leadership opportunities during high school and college years can be a very effective way to prepare for career success. A person who organizes a band gets valuable experience in motivating other band members, in planning, and problem solving, plus gains financial and social rewards. The quarterback of an intramural football team makes decisions on who to rely on with each play he calls. If the game is won, the whole team feels good about their efforts, and the win is evidence of the success of the leader—the quarterback. If a game is lost, the quarterback analyzes, reflects, and identifies lessons to apply in the next game.

We can't all be quarterback or president of the high school band, but there are lots of opportunities for those willing to volunteer and contribute their time and effort in exchange for accumulating valuable experiences.

Phil decided to major in chemical engineering at

college—a logical choice for a kid who grew up in the Texas oil patch, and as a recommendation from a high school counselor. After a month or two of classes, he realized that he was not as well prepared as he had hoped and was having a particularly rough time with calculus. By the time he traveled home for Thanksgiving in his freshman year, he was worried that he might flunk out. But he kept at it, and eventually something clicked and he was able to succeed in calculus class. Phil went on to graduate with a bachelor's degree, followed by a Master of Science in chemical engineering.

He never had a specific career goal—he believed that if he did well in school he could find a job with a big company, earn a good salary, and do well. During summers, while he was in college and graduate school, Phil worked wherever he could to earn a buck. He was a laborer at a grain elevator, the toughest, most miserable job he ever had. He was also a surveyor's helper, and a door-to-door encyclopedia salesman, an unsuccessful experience that convinced him he was not a natural salesman.

Phil was a member of the Army Reserve Officers Training Corps (ROTC) in college, and when he finished his master's studies he was commissioned a second lieutenant and had another win—because of his chemical engineering degrees, he was assigned to Jet Propulsion Lab (JPL) in Pasadena, California. At JPL he conducted research in solid rocket fuels, and he learned to love southern California. He remembers that as an idyllic time—working in a prestigious scientific lab environment, living independently, and learning lots of new things, like computers.

When his army obligation had been satisfied in 1965, he went to work for IBM in Los Angeles as a systems engineer, and was assigned to the oil company accounts, Getty Oil and Texaco. He enjoyed his work at IBM. The technical content of the job was in line with his academic experience, and he also applied the analytical methods and problem solving techniques he learned in engineering school.

It is important to understand that the typical college graduate in 1965 had no computer experience and probably had no detailed understanding of how a computer might be used in a business. That was years before home computers or PCs, and only the largest corporations could afford computers, and the staff to operate them. Phil joined IBM in the early days of the computer revolution, and although he didn't know much about computers when he started, he was a good student and he learned fast.

In addition to learning computer engineering skills, Phil's training at IBM was very important for his personal development, especially learning how to operate in team environments, working on group projects, and learning how to make presentations to a group. The experience helped him develop confidence in his ability to speak in public and lead teams as a manager later in his career.

In 1981, Phil left IBM and went to work for ARCO Products Planning Group, where he worked on marketing support to a group of more than 1,500 ARCO service stations. He was promoted to manage a programming group and found that he enjoyed the management role. He took advantage of an ARCO program that supported higher education and enrolled in Pepperdine University's night school MBA program. He enjoyed the classes, and believes that his second master's degree was a good investment for his management career.

When asked what he would recommend to others interested in preparing for a successful career in management and leadership roles, Phil answers:

> Stretch yourself. Get into leadership roles.
> Put yourself out there.

He also credits his managers and colleagues at ARCO with the help and guidance they provided in the form of coaching and mentoring.

Phil retired from ARCO in 1998, but that wasn't the end of his success with the oil company. For several years after his retirement, he managed software development teams at an ARCO refinery in the Los Angeles area on a contract basis as a full-time consultant. This helped build his retirement nest egg, and he enjoyed the project management responsibilities.

At the end of our interview I asked Phil to sum up the most important factors that led to his career success. He said he had a strong inner drive to succeed, and he worked hard on preparing for success, which in his case meant education. He says that his education—his degrees—were the cornerstone of his success. Who can argue with that?

Today Phil and his wife, Aryna, have a total of seven grandchildren who keep them busy and engaged. In addition to his career story, Phil shared his thoughts in a document, *Preparing for a Successful Life,* which follows.

Preparing for a Successful Life

By Phil Caruthers

John Lennon declared in one of his songs, "Life is what happens to you while you're busy making other plans." Life is a bumpy, thrilling ride that is unpredictable. It is very likely that 10 years from now you will be in a situation very different from what you expect.

How do you deal with the unpredictable? And what is success? Personal success is what *you* define it to be, not what other people say. One definition is "feeling good about yourself and your accomplishments."

You will probably set some fuzzy goals, or at least expectations, for yourself. Maybe you will see yourself in a good job, with a nice house, and a family. Maybe you will have dreams of being a big-time movie star, entertainer or sports figure. Possibly you may want to be a great scientist, or author, or head of a big company, or inventor of life-changing inventions.

But how do you get there? What must you do to greatly improve your chances for a successful life? Being prepared for whatever curves and opportunities life throws at you is the basis for a successful life.

Here are five springboards to prepare you to launch into the stratosphere of success:

1. Get the best education you can get. Take education seriously. You are investing in yourself. Do the best you can in each subject, even if you don't see how you will use the subject matter later in life. Your performance (and grades) indicates to colleges and future employers how well-equipped you are to handle whatever is thrown at you; how well you can overcome obstacles; how good a thinker you are; and how versatile you can be at handling a wide range of challenges.

2. Always seek to improve yourself. Stretch yourself. Practice longer than you are supposed to.

Are you nervous about speaking to a group? Take a speech course. Being able to speak to a group is a very powerful skill, and it will build your own confidence.

Worried about asking that person on a date? Be, and act confident. If you are turned down, ask again later.

Fears will remain fears until you confront them. Do something uncomfortable to overcome a fear. Talk to your friends and ask them to help you get elected as a class officer. Try out for a class play.

Read self-improvement books. Look for leadership opportunities. Ask yourself daily, *what can I do today to improve myself,* and spend 15 minutes doing it.

Involve yourself in the community. Look for

opportunities to help those less fortunate than you, or to support a cause that you feel strongly about. Seek a brief interview with a community leader, and find out why he or she is successful, and what advice they can give.

3. Observe others, and cultivate relationships with those you admire. Learn from others. What do they do well, and why? Develop relationships with strong, personable people. Networking can greatly expand your opportunities, and opportunity is a key to success. Many successful careers are based on friendships built in high school and college.

4. Don't make stupid mistakes that could ruin your life. OK, here are the *don'ts*. It is so easy and common to do something out of passion or just "testing the limits" that can ruin you for the rest of your life. Growing up means dealing with very strong urges and peer pressures that encourage you to take big chances. Learn how to say *No–that's not cool, it's dumb,* when your peers say, *Come on you chicken, do it.* This applies to drugs, alcohol, and criminal activities like shoplifting.

An arrest record will follow you for life like a curse.

Don't drive recklessly to show off for your friends. They won't remember you very long after your funeral.

Sex is a big thing that will hang over you constantly. The last thing you need is to deal with an unwanted pregnancy or a sexually transmitted disease. Learn about and practice safe sex when the urge is too overwhelming to resist. Marrying too early can drag you down for the rest of your life, because it creates huge obligations and severely restricts your opportunities for a successful life.

5. Be a "stand up" person. Earn the respect of others by exhibiting strong character. Be truthful, loyal to your friends and family and employer — be honest and don't lie. Be careful about gossiping about people, or believing the gossip that you hear. Certain people like to pull other people down in their misguided belief that it will elevate themselves.

Now, set yourself some goals, prepare, and go out and become the most successful person you can be!

16

Dr. Eric Kvinsland

"It's amazing what you can learn from other people…"

Dr. Eric Kvinsland, not yet in his 40s, is the owner of a dental clinic in Washington State. Eric purchased the practice from his father, Dr. Jon Kvinsland, who started the business 38 plus years ago and still practices dentistry with his son. Eric attended Washington State University, Pacific Lutheran University, and graduated from the University of Washington dental school.

The youngest of three brothers, Eric learned a lot from his older siblings while growing up. He also knew his own mind. He played soccer beginning at age four or five, but after ten years he wound up on a high school team with a coach he didn't care for and, at age 15, quit the team. That same day, he went to the local airport to find out the age requirement to earn a pilot's license. The answer was 16. Instead of waiting, he started and finished his flight school, and at age 16, he earned his license. Like many young men, Eric liked cars, boats, airplanes—"anything with an engine!"—and thought he might become an airline pilot after he finished school. That was not the path he chose, but he still enjoys flying today.

The flight training and earning the license benefitted Eric in several significant ways. First, when he started training at age 15, he was a kid who chose to reach for a very adult goal—to become a pilot. This wasn't simple. He needed to convince his parents, come up with the money—around $3,000 in those days—and make a commitment to become a very good pilot. As he said, if you are not able to focus on the goal of becoming an excellent pilot and make that your commitment, then you don't belong up in the air. You need all the self-confidence you can muster when you are approaching the runway on your first solo landing.

At about the same time he was making a commitment to aviation, Eric also made some choices in his personal life. He was headed for college and thought about becoming a dentist, like his dad. Whatever career he decided to pursue, Eric understood that he would have to prepare by completing college, and perhaps graduate school. He began to follow a different path than some of his high school friends—and he avoided situations where kids focused on drugs and other risky behavior. To pay for his flight time, he worked part-time at the local airport, refueling planes and doing odd jobs. These pursuits pulled him away from some friends, and he used his pilot's status to fend off others who were experimenting with drugs—he told them he would jeopardize his pilot's license if he used drugs. It was an effective antidote to the negative peer pressure.

Eric studied business at Washington State University, where he met his wife-to-be, Bradie. After graduation, he left the Northwest for California, where he settled in Santa Monica and pursued a career in acting. One of his brothers was a successful actor and lighting specialist, but Eric found that a Hollywood career was not the best fit for him. He had always been impressed with his father's career in dentistry. Dr. Kvinsland made a good living, was known and respected in the community, and was recognized as an outstanding dentist by his peers.

Eric liked the fact that his dad was his own boss, ran his own business, and was dedicated to helping people with their health care. He liked the idea of working with his hands, acquiring valuable skills, and helping patients correct and prevent problems.

Becoming a dentist was an attractive career, but Eric was concerned that he would have to put in another six or seven years of school to earn his dentist license. He needed a couple of years of science classes to earn admission to dental school, and four years to complete his basic professional training. He looked around for other career options and one day found himself with an appointment with the CEO of Helly Hansen, the Scandinavian sportswear manufacturer.

He described the meeting.

> I met with the president of Helly Hansen about a potential job. I loved the outdoors and figured this guy had it made. He asked me what job I would want in the company. Honestly, I told him *his* job. He told me he had no doubt I could get there and then told me about how he had worked as a janitor for the company for 10 years, and then was hired as a sales associate for the next 20 years, where he worked nights, weekends and holidays. And now, he said, he had the perfect job. He told me that everyone puts in their time at some point. You either grind your way through to get to be the CEO or you go to school to learn a trade or profession.
>
> He knew I had considered dental school and he grilled me on that career path. His advice was for me to go to dental school and take over our family business. It was great advice and I have never regretted it.

Eric returned to Washington and enrolled in Pacific Lutheran University to earn the science credits for dental school. After two years, he was ready to apply and it turned out that he was accepted at three top-rated schools, including his first choice, the University of Washington. At about this time, he and Bradie had rekindled their relationship and they decided to marry and raise a family.

Dental students were not allowed to work while school was in session. To supplement Bradie's income as a Child Life Specialist at Swedish Hospital, Eric financed dental school with student loans, and during the summers, helped manage the local airport, and also worked as a deckhand on fishing boats in Alaska during two seasons. One thing he learned in Alaska was that fishing was hard, dangerous, and punishing work—not a career option for him.

Eric did well in dental school, earned an award for restorative dentistry, and graduated in four years. He joined his father in the family business as an associate. He spent a lot of time observing his dad as he practiced his profession and interacted with patients. His dad spent a lot of time teaching Eric the ropes, mentoring him.

After about two years of apprenticeship, Eric was having lunch with a dentist friend, who asked when he was planning to buy his father's practice.Eric replied, "When I think I am ready."

His friend said, "I think you're ready now."

Eric thought about it for a while, then decided to commit to move forward and buy his dad's practice. He was ready to climb into the pilot's seat, grab the controls, and take off. Eric was not yet 30 years old when he bought the dental clinic and began running the practice. His dad was there to help and continued to coach and mentor, but Eric was responsible for retaining the valuable client relationships; paying the rent; hiring and training the staff; paying off his graduate school loans; paying off the note to his father for the practice purchase; keeping up with his professional education; and volunteering his time to community service and to the county and state dental associations.

Although he valued the professional mentoring he

received from his dad, he also had some anxieties about the risks of failure, of harming the practice his father created over three decades.

Eric identified the experiences that contributed to his work ethic, self-reliance, and the confidence to make a go of the professional opportunity to own and manage an established business.

> I would say one of the largest contributors to any success I have been able to obtain was the work ethic lessons from my father. We grew up in a family where my dad was a successful dentist and my mom was a dental hygienist. Though we probably had plenty of resources, we were not aware of them. My dad never gave us handouts—still doesn't.
>
> From a very young age we had to work a certain number of hours in various jobs around the house. We were expected to do our work before we could play or go out. And work didn't mean just working, it meant getting the job done correctly. We then were required to submit a bill to my dad's office and we would be paid with the rest of the employees on the 15th of the month.
>
> If we needed money before that, we should have thought of that last month. There were no loans or extra spending money. If we wanted to go to the movies, we had better think ahead. My brothers and I hated this growing up. Our friends didn't have to do this. But my dad had no room for complaining, so we

accepted our fate. In fact, complaining got you a job raking our beach of large rocks for free. Hard work was drilled into us.

Now my brothers and I are grateful for the lessons this taught us about hard work, and we often joke about my dad getting around child labor laws.

These lessons continued throughout our childhood and high school. If we wanted a car or a boat, he would loan us half and we would pay the other half. When we sold the boat or car, he would get his half first, which sometimes left us with nothing. It taught us to avoid impulses, and really research what we wanted and if it was worth it. We forewent many poor purchases because it would have been a waste of our money. The lessons learned that apply to my life today are endless.

I learned early on that my parents' friends had some great advice if you asked. I wanted to be successful in business—whatever that was going to be—and I knew that listening to their stories could help me in my own journey. They had successful businesses, so I listened to what they would talk about. They weren't perfect, and many parts of their lives I didn't want for myself, but I was able to glean what I felt were the pearls.

What is interesting is I remember writing off some of my parents' friends because they didn't have a magic bullet that got them to where they were. It took me a while to listen to them when they told me

> hard work got them there and then proceeded to tell me about the long and bumpy road they had to success. That is not what I was hoping for.

Early in life, Eric learned an important lesson about people—they like to talk about themselves. They enjoy telling their stories.

As Eric said, "I have many great stories from conversations that I have had with successful people I have met. The honest conversations about real life from people who have checked their ego at the door and will tell you the truth are the best. It's amazing what you can learn from people when you are genuinely interested and listen. I have never learned anything special from listening to myself talk."

Eric learned to ask questions to start the dialog, then sit back and listen. This is something anyone can learn to do, and you can practice and build your skills by talking with relatives, strangers sitting next to you on an airplane, classmates, or just about anywhere. Ask questions, such as where they live, what they do, why they chose that path, what was the proudest moment of their career, or on the playing field.

Talking with Eric produced additional insights into his early experiences that helped prepare him for his successful career. In high school, he volunteered for community service and mentoring/ coaching roles with younger students. He consciously tried to learn from his mistakes, and he sought to develop a leadership style that was similar, in some ways, to his father's leadership style, but not identical—not a copy of his father.

A central concept of Eric's approach to leadership is to treat people the way you would like to be treated.

He also read a lot of books about business and management. One of the most valuable was "Raving Fans: A Revolutionary Approach to Customer Service" by Kenneth Blanchard, whose message applies to almost any career one might choose.

When I asked Eric for one piece of advice that he thought would be helpful to people starting their careers, he responded, "Figure out the person you want to be, then stick with that, no matter what others are doing."

Good advice.

18

Don Lyle

Early Adopter and Tech Wizard

After he completed the seventh grade in Harrisburg, Pennsylvania, Don Lyle and his family moved to Beaumont, Texas, where he finished high school in 1958 and began his career as an electrical engineering student and technologist.

Don described the beginning of his journey.

> I was second in the birth order with one older sister and a younger brother and sister. My parents expressed no strong preference for my continuing education. I think it was assumed that once I completed high school, I'd support myself and make my own decisions.
>
> On graduation I couldn't afford to go to college

> full time—no parental financial assistance was offered or assumed—so I got a job and went to night school at Lamar State College of Technology, majoring in electrical engineering. I went to Lamar for four years—all but two semesters at night; the other two semesters were during the day while I worked thirty hours per week.

Don was interested in electronics, and he also enjoyed science fiction, so enrolling in an electrical engineering course of study was a logical choice. The job he landed turned out to be a wonderful opportunity for Don to learn and, in short order, to become an expert at applying computer technology at a time when most college students had never seen a computer.

(Note: In 1958 young people Don's age were fascinated by transistor radios; Sputnik, the first orbiting satellite; cars with stereos and four-on-the-floor stick shifts; and the Xerox copier and the IBM Correcting Selectric typewriter were considered high technology in the workplace.)

Don described his first job following high school graduation:

> I was fortunate in the employment that I found right out of high school in 1958—I had applied to every place that I could think of, and I received an offer as an "engineering helper" from Gulf States Utilities company, the regional electric utility. I learned almost as much electrical engineering at Gulf States

as I did at Lamar. I was also fortunate in that GSU had a computer in the basement that was used by the accounting department.

I knew of computers from my love of science fiction, so I went down to see it and got fascinated by all the flashing lights. I painfully taught myself to program it and began implementing programs to solve repetitive problems that I encountered in my assigned job. As a result, I became my department's acknowledged computer expert and programmer.

It will certainly sound strange, even quaint, to readers who have grown up with personal computers and smart phones, but in the late 1950s, apps for computers didn't exist. Computers just sat in their temperature controlled, raised floor computer rooms and blinked their lights at you until you figured out how to create a program to make the beast earn its keep.

The earliest machines, like the one Don worked on, were programmed using assembly language, an unfriendly, non-intuitive programming language described by Wikipedia, in part, as follows: "An assembler is a program which creates object code by translating combinations of mnemonics and syntax for operations and addressing modes into their numerical equivalents. This representation typically includes an operation code (opcode) as well as other control bits. The assembler also calculates constant expressions and resolves symbolic names for memory locations and other entities. The use of symbolic references is a key feature of assemblers, saving tedious calculations and manual address updates after program modifications. Most assemblers also include macro facilities for performing textual substitution—e.g., to generate common short sequences of instructions as inline, instead of called subroutines."

To some, programming in assembler was something like trying to ride a zebra—if you ever tried it you would understand why many believed it was impossible. Don had a passionate interest in computers and making them work, and he was willing to work hard and set challenging goals for himself. As an engineering helper, he had a weekly task that consisted of a tedious and repetitive calculation that took him half a day to complete. He knew that computers were designed to perform just this type of task, so he set out to write a program to make these calculations every week.

When Don succeeded in completing the programming, he coded up his input data on punched cards, fed the cards into the computer's card reader, watched the console lights blink for a few minutes, and then stood there amazed as the computer punched out a new set of cards containing the results of the calculations. Accomplishing this goal set Don apart from his peers and ahead of his college classmates, and he was off and running on his career as a technologist, electrical engineer and computer wizard.

Don described how business travel while at Gulf States led to the next chapter in his career:

> Twice each year, I would travel with a group from our department to Texas A&M University to rent time on

> their "big" computer to solve problems larger and more complex than the ones our machine at Gulf States could handle. TAMU had an active program in power engineering, so I met several people who shared my interest in applying digital computers to the solution of power systems problems.
>
> In 1962, TAMU offered me a job continuing my development of programs to solve power-system problems. I also ran a one-man "service bureau" renting time on the TAMU computer to power companies that came to A&M to make use of the programs that I had developed.
>
> It was not unusual for A&M's data processing center to realize between $25K and $50K in revenue each month from this activity.

Four years out of high school, working full-time and attending Lamar Tech, Don had established himself as a computer application software specialist and an engineer who understood complex power systems. His accomplishments in those four years are simply amazing, and based on his own recollections, three major drivers helped him get off to such a blazing start on his career:

1. Don was working in a field—digital computing—that passionately interested him. He had a hands-on opportunity in a new industry where there wasn't a great deal of science yet, where programmers who could make computers perform useful tasks were rare and wonderful—like NBA centers or NFL quarterbacks. You didn't need a PhD to get a

job as a programmer; you just needed to be able to produce useful applications.

2. He worked really hard—head down and focused on his goals. He got a lot done in a short period of time, and his software worked.

3. Don was motivated by a deep insecurity—if he didn't bust his butt on each project, if he didn't meet the ambitious goals he set for himself, someone else would come along and beat him out.

I have talked with sports stars, in particular a long-time NBA center, who have said much the same thing. Each year at the pre-season training camp, talented and hungry young rookies were focused on beating out the veterans and taking their jobs. That kind of pressure and competition tends to clear the mind and helps a person focus on doing their very best on the task at hand. At least, that's how it worked for Don.

The next stage of Don's career is tied to a piece of history—a power grid failure. Here is his account:

> In 1965, the infamous *Northeast Blackout* occurred, subjecting much of the northeastern United States to a power outage of several hours duration. People were outraged and a congressional investigation ensued. The northeastern inter-connected utilities hired a major engineering consulting firm, Stone & Webster in Boston, to investigate the disturbance, determine its cause(s), and recommend solutions. Stone & Webster retained me to provide simulations

> of the event, since I had developed a computer program capable of simulating the effects of such events on power systems. I took a leave of absence from A&M and lived in Boston during late 1965 and early 1966 working on this problem.

Don met Stone & Webster employees while working on simulation software at Texas A&M. Soon after finishing his simulation assignments for Stone & Webster, he accepted a programmer position at Burroughs Corporation. He was extremely impressed with the design of Burroughs' new computers, and wanted to write software that could take advantage of the new machines. Don learned a lot on the job. By observing his colleagues and making good use of advice from more experienced managers, he worked his way up the ladder into executive positions.

He explained how it happened:

> I joined Burroughs to write compilers. After about a year, I was running the compiler group; then I was lured away to run a department that was responsible for the engineering and manufacturing automation software. The systems software group got into trouble and I was brought back to a position that Burroughs called Activity Manager, a position in which all of the systems software departments reported to me.
>
> The most significant positions that I held were probably with Burroughs Corporation (now Unisys)

where I advanced from a programming position to one of running a multi-national manufacturing and engineering group employing thousands of people. I also held vice president positions such as VP of Systems Management and VP of Advanced Technology for the company.

I didn't set out to be an executive—I just wanted to be the best engineer/programmer that I could be. It was actually a surprise to me when a management position was first offered. Leadership ability wound up being important to my success, although it was first expressed as technology leadership—changing the direction of technical projects through persuasive technical arguments.

I had one mentor in particular at Burroughs who told me when I was a fairly low-level manager that I should think of my career in terms of reaching the top, or very near the top, of the corporation. It was the first time I had ever thought in those terms. He also gave me opportunities to take on big challenges and provided me with a sounding board for my thoughts on solutions to knotty management problems. I learned something about management and motivating people from every boss I ever had—in some cases I learned what NOT to do.

Developing a new computer system can be an enormous and costly project, in many ways similar to the massive efforts necessary to develop a new airplane, such as Boeing's

Dreamliner, or to construct a subway system like BART in San Francisco or WMATA in Washington D.C. In the early 1960s when IBM announced the System 360 family of computers, Fortune magazine published a story describing the projects development cost, $5 billion, as the most expensive corporate development project in history.

They also described the System 360 project as a "you bet your company" decision. Big projects usually call for multiple high-performing teams—design teams, development teams, test team —whose work is interdependent. The success of the entire project depends on the success of each team.

The development team needs the output of the design team to begin their work. The test team needs the prototype version of the product to begin testing. Teams that produce useful results on schedule help the project along. Teams that fall behind schedule or fail to meet performance objectives hurt the project. Successful businesses, especially technology businesses, spend a lot of time and effort studying high-performing teams trying to figure out what makes them tick.

How do you develop, motivate and manage high-performing teams? I talked with Don about this topic and he described one of his experiences managing a development team at Burroughs that was in trouble.

> I once led a team that accomplished near miracles. We were working on a computer system that had fallen hopelessly behind schedule and I was brought in to fix the problems. I had joined this group because they had a reputation in the industry for

> "walking on water" and yet this major project was failing. I managed to motivate them by shaming them—throwing up their previous reputation to them and telling them that the group had become the laughing stock of the corporation.
>
> We committed ourselves to doing whatever it took to turn things around and we did so, re-establishing the group's reputation.

After sixteen years with Burroughs, Don retired, but he remained active in the technology business by serving as an outside director on corporate boards of several dozen technology companies. He enjoyed coaching CEOs, who were often fellow tech wizards, and his experience and advice was a valuable contribution to these companies. By early 2015, Don stepped down from most of the corporate boards, but he is still an active director for several boards connected to higher education. He remains highly interested in technology that he considers interesting or significant, and he is a leading "early adopter".

When I visited Don and his lovely wife Maryann in April 2015, they were both wearing Apple watches complementing their iPhones, and he was driving his second Tesla, equipped with a button to trigger "insane acceleration"—zero to sixty in three seconds flat. A dozen years ago, Don emailed me the first photo I had ever seen taken and transmitted over the Internet by a smart phone. I have never met another person who seems to enjoy technology as much as Don does.

I'll end this chapter with other bits of advice from Don on preparing for career success:

> I strongly recommend that young people earn their own spending money. It encourages a strong work ethic and teaches valuable skills.
>
> It is considered unusual for technical people to be able to express themselves well in speech and/or writing. Both of these skills are essential for leaders. Take courses in speech and emphasize good spelling and grammar in written communications. Learn how to make an effective presentation.
>
> If you enjoy what you do, you don't need to work a day in your life.

19

Kent Weymouth

A Bumpy Road

Kent and Sally Weymouth live in a lovely new home in a community of other lovely new homes in South Carolina. They moved a few years ago from the Philadelphia area, looking for a location closer to kids and grandkids, and which offered milder weather and more golf. Sally is a regular competitor on the golf club circuit, and Kent now has a second career as a starter at a municipal course one day a week, which compensates him with free golf whenever he wants to play. In 2014, they traveled to Europe and Alaska, and Kent is usually working on plans for the next trip. They lead a good life and enjoy it to the hilt, especially the family get-togethers they organize every few years.

Kent had a very successful career in the investment

business, but there were a lot of roadblocks and setbacks. I have known him for more than fifty years and when I interviewed him for this book, I kept coming back to the same conclusion—he succeeded because he is independent; is willing to make tough decisions and stick with them; and he was determined to become successful and to work hard to make it happen despite numerous obstacles.

Kent was popular while in high school in Maryland, and a very good student. He played on the football and golf teams, and was a regular participant at the weekly quarter-limit poker games, where many of the guys puffed on evil-smelling cigars, like Rum River Crooks and Swisher Sweets. He also organized and managed an investment club with a dozen or so members. Both of his parents were college graduates and when Kent, the oldest of four children, graduated from high school, it was expected that he would go to college. He enrolled at the University of Maryland.

With no specific career goals or direction, he found it difficult to concentrate on academic life. He attended Maryland for two years, but felt increasingly aimless and lost interest in college. Kent left the university, found a job at the local electric utility company, and took courses at the junior college. The job didn't work out, and the junior college program didn't inspire him. At this point in his life, he believed he didn't have very many options.

Like any young man 18 years of age or older in the early 1960s, Kent was likely to be drafted into the Vietnam war if he was no longer a full-time college student, which he definitely was not. So Kent made a decision about his future—he enlisted in the U.S. Navy.

Kent's dad was a civilian employee of the Navy, but he was not happy with his son's decision. Nevertheless, Kent followed through and spent two years in the Navy, including shipboard service on an aircraft carrier in the Mediterranean. His time in the Navy was a great experience— "…what I needed at that stage," he explained. Early in his enlistment, he decided to apply for Officer Candidate School so he could learn to fly. The application process included a number of tests and somewhere along the line Kent didn't do well on a test, so that option became closed to him.

In time, he understood more and more about the different and more desirable lives the officers lived compared to the enlisted sailors, and he developed a very clear idea of how he wanted to live once he finished his time in the Navy. He wanted to be a success, and a person in control of his own life, and not a person controlled by others.

Despite the disappointment of not being able to qualify for officers school and flight training, Kent found a lot to like during his service in the Navy. He traveled around the country and the Mediterranean region, and found that he enjoyed visiting new places and meeting new people. He knew that when he got out of the service he would return to college and complete his college degree, so he saved money and earned extra cash by running a discreet loan service for his colleagues. If a sailor needed to borrow $4.00 the day before payday, he could get a loan from Kent, then pay him back with interest the next day. The time in the Navy was a good experience.

The fact that Kent hadn't succeeded in his first try at college—or in his desire to learn to fly and become a Navy officer — did not weigh on him as failures or serious threats to his goals of a successful career and a good life. With his savings from his Navy pay and financial support from the G.I. bill, he was ready to start and eager to finish college as quickly as he could.

The University of Maryland would not allow Kent to enroll again until he proved himself by getting good grades at some other institution. So he attended American University in Washington, D.C. for a year, did well, then transferred to Maryland to finish a degree in business and finance. He was in a rush to finish his undergraduate classes and get on with life, so he took 18 to 20 hours of classes each semester, and earned a bachelor's degree in two and a half years after his discharge from the service.

With degree in hand, he went searching for a job and found one at a Westinghouse Electric facility near Baltimore in their finance and accounting group. He described the work as sitting at a desk in a cubicle in a huge room filled with junior accountants like himself, all posting numbers and producing accounting reports. After six months, Kent decided that this job was not going to lead to the success he wanted, and he left.

Next he talked to Merrill Lynch about becoming a stock broker, but he didn't do well on the sales aptitude tests so that didn't go anywhere. He joined Burroughs Corporation and spent a couple of years selling accounting machines.

It was at this point in his life that he met, fell in love

with and married Liz, a lovely young woman who was just finishing up her studies to become a teacher. He also developed a much clearer vision of his career goal. He decided that he would become an investment analyst—a specialist who would invest client's money and earn a living from fees. This played well with his interest in business and finance and his desire to be in control. As an analyst, he would conduct the research, study the companies and their performance, and make recommendations based on his own work and analysis.

It all sounded good. His goal was aligned with his interests and aptitudes, but there was one significant obstacle. If he wanted to become an investment analyst, or more specifically, if he wanted an investment company to hire and give him a chance to become an analyst, he needed a a master's degree in finance. Kent decided to go for it and when Liz graduated and started teaching, he resigned from Burroughs to pursue an MBA at Maryland. He completed his studies in three semesters, and with his advanced degree in hand, he updated his resume, made 100 copies to prospective employers, and waited for lightning to strike.

This was the beginning of the decade of the 1970s and the economy was in the dumper. Ninety-nine of those prospective employers did not think hiring Kent Weymouth was the most important thing they could do to turn things around. But one company did respond, and Kent soon had an offer to join the investment department of Monumental Life, an insurance company headquartered in Baltimore, Maryland. His starting salary was not impressive, but the decision was an easy one—he had no other good option. So he took the job and spent the next five years at Monumental, learning the ins and outs of private placement investments.

Private placements are institutional investments, often made by banks and insurance companies to generate profits from their deposited cash. The borrowers are often businesses who find private placement loans more attractive or more available than the alternative of raising cash by selling bonds or selling stock shares in a public offering.

Kent's job was to analyze the prospective borrowers, study their track records and their business plans, then decide whether each deal looked like a good deal for Monumental. It was complicated business, but he learned fast and did well. To expand his knowledge of the investment business, Kent studied for and received his Chartered Financial Analyst (CFA) designation.

A small community of financial experts manage most of the private placement investments for large institutional investors, and over time Kent got to know quite a few. After five years learning the business and doing deals for Monumental Life, an acquaintance at Penn Mutual offered Kent a job. It was a larger pond, a chance to do bigger deals—a major step ahead. He signed on to Penn Mutual and he and Liz, now with two young sons, moved to Pennsylvania.

Kent was doing well at Penn Mutual. Life was good. Then, without warning, came terrifying news. Liz was diagnosed with leukemia. They tried every kind of treatment, including a bone marrow transplant. Penn Mutual was extremely supportive and understanding. But nothing stopped the deadly progress of the disease and Liz died, tragically, in 1980, leaving Kent to cope with two boys, eight and six years old, who had lost their mother. As Kent said, all plans were disrupted. He was frantically trying to hang on at work as he struggled to help his sons with their grief, to help them understand the terrible loss of their mother, help them deal with life every day. It was all just too much, and as he struggled and floundered he began to realize that what he was trying to do was not an option—he needed to make a change in his career and find the control he wanted in life.

In 1984, Penn Mutual was in the process of down-sizing and Kent was let go. Penn Mutual was supportive and he left with a good separation packagethat allowed him to start over. Kent chose a new path towards being his own boss, doing his own thing. He went into business as a fee-only financial advisor, focusing on young, middle-income careerists who needed help with strategies and tactics to build enough wealth to enjoy their 70th birthday parties. Unlike most financial planners, he didn't earn commissions on stocks, mutual funds, or insurance he recommended; he only earned a fee, established up front.

He worked hard to build his credentials and his knowledge of the investment planning business, and he earned the Chartered Financial Consultant (ChFC) designation. He worked a lot of hours, required to prepare and present a financial plan for each client.

Because he was working with younger people with modest incomes, his fees were small. Although his first attempt at starting his own business was not a financial success, he did meet, and married, a wonderful woman, Sally, who had two young daughters.

The next stage of Kent's career was a large step ahead. He joined a financial advisor firm as a partner, with the prospect of becoming an owner of a significant piece of the business. However, the deal did not work out. After the first couple of years, as he began to work out the details of acquiring substantial ownership of the business, it became clear that he was not going to get as big of a piece of the action as he believed he had earned.

Once more, he looked at his options and decided that the best choice was to remain on the job until he could save up enough cash to support himself and his family while he started up his own firm. He would save enough money to cover living expenses and business expenses for eighteen months to two years. Once he had his start-up capital, he would quit. And he did, after five years with the company.

It was a lot harder than he thought it would be. In addition to starting his own firm, he now had a larger family to consider. He had made some big investments in his future—a college degree, an MBA, nearly twenty years of experience, his CFA and ChFC designations—and now he was looking for the payoff.

Kent found it in the form of the Pennsylvania Teachers' Pension Fund, which managed the investment of all the funds set aside to pay retirement pensions to Pennsylvania teachers once they qualified for retirement benefits. The Pension Fund wanted to invest some of their assets—$500 million to be exact—in private placement investments, and they issued a public Request for Proposal (RFP) inviting interested and qualified parties to submit proposals for managing the investments.

Kent was extremely interested and believed he was well-qualified. It was hard to imagine a better opportunity. He had an excellent pedigree in private placements, and the Teachers' Pension Fund was a huge prospective client. If he could win this business, his agency would experience instant success. He did his homework, spent time getting to know the managers at the Fund, and wrote the best proposal he could. He realized he would be competing with all the big investment banks, so his strategy was to bid low. He bid very low.

He received a phone call from the Chief Investment Officer, a person Kent had come to know while preparing the proposal. Another agency had followed the same strategy, and offered to do the work for less money. The selection board had chosen the lowest bidder. Kent was out.

During that same phone call, Kent asked a few questions. Did the Fund intend to give the chosen agency the entire $500 million? Would it not be more prudent to split the money between two different investment advisors? If Kent cut his fees to equal the successful bid, would the Fund give him a portion of the money to invest?

The Fund liked the sound of his reasoning, and decided to do exactly what Kent suggested. He started out managing half the assets—$250 million—and before long saw that grow to $350 million. His first three years, the length of the initial contract he signed, showed that he could meet their objectives and more. He and Fund management negotiated contracts in which Kent received performance bonuses.

Over the years, a number of the investments Kent made for the Fund were very successful and his firm flourisehd. He was able to retire early and moved to South Carolina, where he and Sally enjoy travel and activities with their family of fifteen kids and grandkids.

I asked Kent what made him successful.

> Stick-to-it-tiveness. Support from family. And the ability to adjust to life-changing circumstances.

I would add determination and independence. Nothing was handed to him, and few things came easy. On a number of occasions during his life when he tried to move forward, he chose the wrong path and had to backtrack. When there were failures, he dusted himself off and moved on. He faced the tragedy of his first wife's fatal illness, and the impossible burden of raising his sons while pursuing a career.

Kent not only invested in his future by earning degrees and designations, he earned the money to pay for them. There is never a guarantee of a payoff in investments. That's where his determination and decision to become independent made a difference.

It begins to sound like a broken record: if you pursue a career you enjoy and you are willing to work hard and make the necessary investments, and you have the determination to succeed, you probably will.

20

What Do These Stories Tell Us?

One thing that should be clear by now is that there are many paths to success. The collection of real life stories and my commentary, presented as a sort of career buffet, provides the opportunity to browse and sample the experiences of 17 successful people whose stories may help you navigate your own career path. They gave their best advice to help others achieve success.

Another important lesson we can learn from these stories is that not everyone has the same opportunities. Jim Burns and Eric Kvinsland decided to pursue family businesses. For Buzz Curry, C.J. Berwick, Don Lyle and most of the others this wasn't an option. Any reader who has the opportunity to enter a family business should pay close attention to Jim and Eric's stories. They both worked hard preparing to start their careers and they both risked highly visible and painful failures if they proved unable to keep the businesses growing. They both succeeded, but may have had a few nights when their sleep was troubled by concerns for their enterprises.

Jim and Eric made successes out of their family businesses, but many second-generation business leaders fail. In every case I have examined, success in carrying on a family enterprise is earned through careful preparation, hard work, and successful mentoring. Taking over the family business is rarely a slam-dunk.

A few contributors started out with a well-defined goal, or at least a direction in mind, and worked hard to make it happen. Coach Bill Brown is an outstanding example—head football coach in a Southern California high school. Changed his first name to Coach.

C.J. tells us that she always wanted to be in the hospitality business, and when she saw the chance she grabbed it. Don Lyle was fascinated by computers, technology and science, and he was driven to creating the best software for the best computers he could find. Kent Weymouth had to juggle a lot to overcome serious setbacks, but he always seemed to gravitate towards finance and investing. Beginning with his high school investment club and loan-sharking in the Navy, he wound up running hundreds of millions of dollars in private placement investments for the Pennsylvania Teachers pension funds.

If you think you know your career goal, or the general area you want to explore, spend some time figuring out the preparation and pre-requisites and then go for it!

Most of us spend the years between our early 20s and the end of our 30s learning and perfecting our skills. By our 40s and 50s, if we are successful, we have learned most of what we need to know for the rest of our careers. We have earned a reputation—a good one, we hope—and we have accumulated enough experience to develop good judgment and problem solving skills

If you agree with this very rough timeline, then you will probably agree that the first dozen or so years on the job should ideally be in a good learning environment. In my experience, large organizations—whether they be the U. S. Army or Air Force, Burroughs, IBM, Amazon, Starbucks, or the federal government—offer excellent training, advancement opportunities, and often they will pay for advanced degrees, as noted in the career stories of Buzz Curry, George Babbitt, and Phil Caruthers. George didn't set out to become a career officer, but as time passed and his career progressed, he found success, opportunity, and rewards that kept him engaged and motivated until retirement.

Jake Culp thrived in the Federal Government Management Intern program. Phil Caruthers enjoyed a successful career beginning with the Army, then IBM, then Arco. Aryna Swope and Gloria Burgess both started their careers within large organizations. Kent Weymouth only served one hitch in the Navy, but he said he learned a lot and enjoyed his time there, and the experience enabled him to make plans for a rewarding future career.

The point here is that a large organization can be a good

place to start a career, and if you find a good fit, it could be a good place to finish one up, as well.

As discussed, to achieve success requires academic preparation, finding a field or an environment that you are passionate about, developing talents and skills, and effective mentoring, but no book about career success would be complete without a few words on the topic of reputation.

Buzz hit the bullseye when he said that one of the most important attributes that the senior level promotion boards considered was reputation. This doesn't have much to do with whether you were a Marshall Scholar or Harvard MBA. It has *everything* to do with how colleagues and senior management view you, what they think of you, whether you are on the good-guy list. You know who the good guys are. They are the colleagues you trust. The people who are always willing to help, to go the extra mile. The ones who know and care about the goals of the organization they are part of. The people who are obviously busting their butts to do a superior job on the task at hand.

These are the people who have earned good reputations in their work environment, and who, in time, are rewarded, promoted, and respected. They are usually positive, hard-working, generous to others, and they often start out by being role models for more junior folks. Find them and emulate them and you will increase your chances for success.

After compiling the 17 career stories for this book, I read through them to extract common themes for advice, and also identified what the contributors said about skills and habits that were most important, in their minds.

The Top 5 recurring themes:

1. Invest in education and preparation. Fifteen out of 17 contributors referred to the need for specific, usually academic, preparation.

2. Mentors. Fifteen contributors pointed out the value of effective mentors.

3. Hard work. Fourteen talked about the importance of hard work, including Don Lyle who taught himself how to make that first computer do tricks; or Buzz's advice to "bust your butt on the job you've got."

4. Choose a career you care about—a career that inspires your passion.

5. Look for volunteer opportunities, on the job or elsewhere, that build skills and experience.

The next six are also important:

Setbacks. Ten of the contributors described significant setbacks that confronted them—knockdowns that were serious problems at the time, but problems they overcame.

Leadership. Ten stressed the importance of cultivating leadership skills.

Confidence. Ten spoke of the importance of finding experiences that build confidence.

Set goals. Nine contributors thought this was an important habit to develop.

Take risks; try new things. This was emphasized by seven.

Public speaking skills and writing skills were considered important. If you learn how to communicate effectively with individuals and groups—in writing, conversation, and presentations—you will find these to be valuable skills in your career, and throughout your personal life.

If you have read this far, you are interested in achieving a successful career. Follows is a series of exercises you can begin, whether you are in high school, college, graduate school, or have already started a career.

First, list a few career choices of interest. Next, conduct a self-assessment to see where you are on developing the skills, talents and experiences that our contributors identified as important for success. List recommendations made by the contributors, and stack-rank the list of skills and experiences so that the ones most important for your career goals are at the top, and less important skills and experiences are at the bottom. Rate yourself on a 1 to 5 scale (5 being all-star, 1 being unskilled). For example, a self-assessment may look something like this:

Skills and experience	Rating
Education / preparation	4
Public Speaking	1
Writing	3
Mentors	2
Leadership	2

Once you have the skills and experience organized with the most important at the top, and each are assessed, you can easily see where your focus should be to strengthen skills or gain more experience. A college engineering student, for example, might have a goal of a career in robotics or composite materials. The education plan could be well developed: complete undergraduate program, earn bachelor's degree; enroll in master of science program at a university recognized for excellence in robotics or composite materials programs. The education and career preparation would assess as a 4, 4.5, or a 5. That's well and good, but looking down the list of skills and experience, that same aspiring engineer might come up with a much lower assessment score on writing or public speaking. A plan should be developed to sharpen skills in communication. The exercise then goes on to develop and execute a skill-building plan.

To summarize, pick a career choice or two; stack-rank the skills and experiences necessary for success in that career with the most important at the top; assess skill level and level of experience; and create a plan with specific goals and a timetable to achieve.

A final thought … It is always good to be prepared. Many companies have organized performance appraisal systems that require managers to assess each employee's performance in writing at least once a year. Many employees see this as a key event in the salary administration process, and it may well be. Not as many junior level employees understand that career planning and preparation is also part of the appraisal process. Most managers are obliged to maintain and update some sort of career plan for each employee. In some cases, especially if the manager involved is inexperienced or overloaded, the career planning may not be very helpful. For example, if you start out at the bottom, say as a junior budget analyst, your manager might get away with a career plan that reads, simply: *Susie is working toward a promotion to associate budget analyst within two to four years*. However, Susie may reach that promotion in two years, rather than four, if the manager helps her define the steps to get there.

Invest some time when preparing for performance appraisals. Take advantage of this opportunity to talk frankly with your manager about your aspirations. Prepare a series of questions and statements that may help you move your career along.

Some examples:

» *Overall, are you and others in this organization satisfied with my performance so far?*

» *In the time that I have been here, I have been very impressed with this organization and I have started thinking about my own career goals within the company. I would like to take steps toward going into management, or becoming a senior engineer, or getting into outside sales, etc.*

» *What should I do over the next twelve months to better prepare for future opportunities?*

Ask questions in a positive, non-threatening way, and begin with acknowledgement that performing well in your current job is the first priority. Discuss career plans and identify clear career goals with your manager to help assist in developing and documenting a career plan for you to follow. Ask your manager to help establish reasonable milestones for you to achieve in the career path to success.

Make it known that you are eager to take on additional responsibilities. Never look at extra tasks or assignments as burdens, but rather as opportunities to show your ability and willingness to help the organization that employs you.

21

Resources

How to Prepare

Hopefully, you will benefit from learning what these seasoned professionals have experienced in real life to accomplish their goals. Although their chosen careers are quite different—from a restaurant owner to a United States Congressman; from a football coach to Army and Air Force Generals—each found ways to strengthen weaknesses, to improve the chances to succeed.

What resources do you have available to help as you travel on the path to success? For starters, the advisors in this book might be considered as early mentors. Look for opportunities to work with mentors in your areas of interest. Apply for intern positions during summer breaks from college, or as part of a university-corporate partnership program.

Many large corporations offer internships for undergraduate and advanced degree programs. The military offers educational opportunities, training in specific careers (for example, aviation), and also provides plenty of options for acquiring leadership, organizational and communication skills.

Find ways to fund your education. Scholarships abound for those who are willing to take the time to find them and to apply. Federal financial aid is not the only resource. Meet with the financial aid office at the college you'd like to attend, or the college advisor at your school. A lot of unusual scholarships are not awarded simply because no one applied — such as, people with a specific last name, or twins. Scholarships are also available for people who excel in chess, table tennis, or have participated in community service. One website with information on finding and applying for scholarships is www.finaid.org/scholarships. Do your research!

Online learning and junior colleges are less expensive options than enrolling in larger universities. Many companies offer tuition reimbursement programs for undergraduate and advanced degrees, including for part-time employees, and with no restrictions for field of study.

How to decide on a career. Again, do your research. The U.S. Bureau of Labor Statistics website has a host of career-specific information on the labor market, including descriptions of various occupations; training and education required; average incomes; and 10-year projections for growth, by career and industry. Information is also available by state and region.
(www.dol.gov/dol/topic/statistics/occupations)

Not enough can be said about the benefits of **giving your time and talents** throughout the community. Most all of the contributors talked about the value of volunteerism, a life-long opportunity to give and to learn. Participate in the endless opportunities to serve, while exploring areas of interest and developing skills. The time spent will help decide if you want to enter into that particular field as a career, and will also help build your resumé and form a network of potential employers.

If academia or athletics is on your list of possible careers, become a tutor at a local school or college. Also, Boys & Girls Clubs and YMCAs open their doors to young students for after-school programs. Volunteer to form and lead a team devoted to special programs, such as writing computer applications, writing fiction, or become involved in drama or dance. Coach or officiate recreational athletics for church youth teams, or the local park commission. Form an intensive workshop to teach computer skills or basketball or baseball. Work with Special Olympics.

Perhaps the legal world sparks your interest. I know a successful partner in a leading Seattle law firm who, as an undergraduate at Cornell, served as a volunteer to visit inmates at the county jail. All he could do for them was to give his time and attention and any advice and encouragement he could muster; but the inmates appreciated having someone to talk to, and the experience helped him make the decision to become a lawyer. You really cannot know the value of experience until you get out there and do it.

Practice leadership skills. Step up to the plate and

offer to organize an activity. Lead a youth group to collect food for the local food bank or deliver meals to the elderly. Organize a used clothing drive. Join and lead a project for Habitat for Humanity. Be a summer camp counselor. Train to become a member of a search and rescue team with local law enforcement agencies or the local Red Cross chapter. Head planning committees or serve as committee chair to organize volunteers at fund-raising events or a 10K running event. And don't forget about opportunities in your current job. Volunteer to lead a planning project for a new product or head a task force to solve an operational issue or quality improvement initiative. Form a committee for a United Way project, community service project, or offer to plan a retirement party.

Improve communication skills. Serve as an officer in your homeowners association. Join a business or trade organization. Become a member of Toastmasters International which, for more than 80 years, has helped people master public speaking and leadership. At the office, present your team's project to management in the next staff meeting.

Publish a blog and update it weekly. Ask a friend to critique each blog post before publishing, and encourage reader feedback and opinions about topics. Take a creative writing or journalism class. Become a freelance writer — submit articles to periodicals, magazines, newsletters, or local newspapers.

Network. Meet-up groups are not just for social networking. There are meet-ups for specific areas of technology, marketing, engineers, architects, entrepreneurs, writers, musicians — if you don't find what you want, form a group for your area of interest. (Internet search *Meet-ups* in your area.) Work for a political campaign. Join an organization for small business owners. Conduct or attend a workshop at a local library, continuing education course at a college, or Chamber of Commerce events.

Be smart about money. All the life-long plans and hard work will pay off only if you include financial planning and make wise financial decisions. At some point our wage-earning life will be behind us. Develop financial plans and goals that will pay off the mortgage during working years, or will allow downsizing to a smaller home during retirement, paid for with the equity from a former home; or a reverse mortgage could finance staying in a current home. Whatever your circumstances or preferences, plan well in advance for a place to live, once the paychecks end.

Consider consulting with a financial planner—the best advice is to start early in your career to establish long-range plans. There is no way to know what life will be like following your 70th birthday. We don't know how long we will be alive, and how our health will be, or what the cost of living will be, with the inevitable but unknown impact of inflation. What is known is that we must be smart enough to establish a plan to follow, then adjust as time goes by.

Suppose you want to accumulate $1 million in savings by the time you retire. Imagine a giant piggy bank that holds four million quarters, and every year you managed to deposit $10,000 in quarters in that bank. How long would it take to fill it up? One hundred years—not a good plan.

Now let's suppose you leveraged your savings by investing $10,000 each year in index funds or Exchange Traded Funds, or some other equity investments, and your portfolio grew at an average of 6% per year. How long would it take to reach $1 million? At the end of 34 years you would have nearly $1,030,000, and more than $600,000 of this sum would be supplied by the 6% average annual growth.

Although 34 years sounds a lot more reasonable than 100 years, setting aside $10,000 per year may not seem reasonable, especially in the early years of your career. It may not even be necessary, if you are one of the dwindling numbers of employees covered by a defined benefit pension plan, one that pays a lifetime retirement benefit. Fewer and fewer jobs today offer lifetime pensions, so for most of us, savings plans will be a requirement if we want to be smiling as we blow out the candles on our 70th birthday cake.

Another element of a smart financial plan is to take full advantage of any employer match for your retirement savings. Some employers match as much as 2.5% of your gross pay, so if you are earning $50,000 a year and have $1,250 deducted each year for your Individual Retirement Account, the employer will match this amount, and your account will receive a total of $2,500. As your career progresses and your earnings increase you should be able to afford to contribute more. With the added leverage of employer contributions, that $1 million, or whatever your personal goal is, may not look so far away.

Other things you can do to bulk up your savings is to earmark a significant part of a working spouse's income for savings. Or when you have a windfall, say an inheritance, don't blow it all on a vacation trip or a Porsche, but sock some of it away in savings. A second job or planning to work past normal retirement age will boost your nest egg. Start saving early, make a good plan, be smart about money, and continue to enjoy life after your career ends

I appreciate the willingness of the contributors to this book to share the solid advice and observations from their life stories.

The important skills, experiences and attributes—hard work, mentors, reputation, choosing a career you are passionate about, acquiring expertise—aren't taught in high school, college, or graduate school. They are obtained from real life experience. Make an extra effort to spend time thinking about your future, pay attention, learn, and build important skills from your own experiences. This book should help.

Explore your interests. Hone your skills. Share your expertise.

Good luck!